Internal Migration Systems in the Developing World

Edited by

Robert N. Thomas
and John M. Hunter

Internal Migration
Systems
in the Developing World
With Special Reference
to Latin America

Schenkman Publishing Co. Cambridge, Massachusetts

Copyright © 1980 by Schenkman Publishing Co.

Library of Congress Cataloging in Publication Data

Main entry under title:
Internal migration systems in the developing world.
1. Migration, Internal—Latin America—Addresses,
essays, lectures. 2. Rural-urban migration—Latin
America—Addresses, essays, lectures. 3. Underdeveloped areas—Migration, Internal—Addresses, essays,
lectures. 4. Underdeveloped areas—Rural-urban
migration—Addresses, essays, lectures. I. Thomas,
Robert N., 1926-   II. Hunter, John Melton,
1928-
HB1990.5.A3I57   301.32'6'091724   79-21875
ISBN 0-8161-8414-3 cloth
ISBN 0-87073-931-X paper

This publication is printed on permanent/durable acid-free paper
MANUFACTURED IN THE UNITED STATES OF AMERICA

To C. W. MINKEL

Colleague, Collaborator, Friend

Contents

Introduction

In August 1974, the Latin American Studies Center at Michigan State University was awarded a grant by the Foreign Languages and Area Studies Division of the Office of Education, Department of Health, Education and Welfare, to produce a series of three courses that would discuss "the impact of the development process on Third World environments." Two courses investigated the impact of the development process on rural and urban environments, respectively, while a third course, "Population, Development, and the Environment," acted as a bridge between the rural and urban courses. This volume stems from the third course, where a number of specialists were invited to bring their expertise to bear on the theme.

The book is organized around the actual migration process. After presenting several migration models, the book looks at the rural generating center, how migrants proceed from the countryside to the city, what happens once migrants settle in the urban center, and what alternate strategies can be employed to divert or stem the flood of migrants. These chapters are followed by case studies of internal migration from Africa, Asia, and Latin America.

Initially, James Zuiches discusses migration theory and presents several basic models to describe the process. This introduction sets the stage for the subsequent chapters, which are based on data from empirical research. For example, the chapter entitled, "Social Implications of Changing Population Patterns: The Case of Rural Depopulation in Colombia," by Ernst C. Griffin and Lynden S. Williams, identifies reasons for rural out-migration and points out the effect this process has on the rural generating centers.

Richard C. Jones looks at internal migration from a perception/behavior viewpoint. How do potential migrants view their "opportunity field," and how does propaganda coming from major cities influence migration streams?

The physical movement from rural to urban centers is presented by

Robert N. Thomas and James L. Mulvihill in the chapter "Temporal Attributes of Stage Migration in Guatemala." How does the typical migrant proceed from a rural home to the bright lights of the urban mecca? What changes have occurred in this process through time?

Stillman and Leila Bradfield approach internal migration from the perspective of the urban receiving center. What effect does the in-pouring of rural people have on the social, economic, and physical composition of the city?

Assuming that something needs to be done to reduce rural–urban migration to Third World cities, the chapter by Barry Lentnek presents alternate strategies that could be employed to stem migrant flows to the principal urban centers of the developing world. What kinds of public and private programs could be initiated to lessen the flow of peasants to the city?

The next three chapters are specific case studies of internal migration systems, using African, Asian, and Latin American examples. J. Barry Riddell looks at an African case in "African Migration and Regional Disparities," Bernard and Rita S. Gallin utilize a case study from Taiwan in their chapter, "The Integration of Village Migrants into Urban Society: The Case of Taipei, Taiwan," and Richard W. and Jane Riblett Wilkie employ an Argentine data set in their chapter, "Migration and a Rural Community in Transition: A Case Study in Argentina," to develop further internal migration theory.

The book represents the work of several disciplines. The editors are a geographer and an economist. And while most of the authors are geographers, the chapters include works by anthropologists and sociologists. All the contributors have done extensive fieldwork in their areas of interest and have contributed numerous works on migration elsewhere.

James J. Zuiches

Migration Methods and Models: A Demographic Perspective*

Introduction

The cross-cultural interaction of population changes with economic and social development is quite apparent, but this interaction is also relevant when the internal relations between the urban–rural or developed–developing sections of any given country are examined. Although the pattern of world population growth has seemingly peaked at 2 percent per annum, variations still exist in country population growth rates, from over 3 percent for selected Latin American countries to near stability (growth rates of 0.4 to 0.1 percent per year) in Western Europe. Internal variations likewise remain. In the United States from 1970 to 1973, metropolitan areas grew 2.9 percent, more slowly than the rural nonmetropolitan areas' growth at 4.2 percent (Beale 1975). But in Latin American countries, urban populations were growing dramatically. In 1975, Mexico City grew 10.9 percent, and São Paulo, Rio de Janeiro, and Buenos Aires grew over 8 percent (Turner 1976). At the same time, the rural population averaged slightly over one percent growth per annum. This measurement of population growth, however, is only the simplest model of the demographic dynamics of a society. It is the purpose of this chapter to elaborate the concept of a population, to describe the measurement of its growth, and to provide the demographic tools for the analysis of that component of total growth that is due to migration.

Migration is an integral part of the history of mankind (Davis 1974). From the treks of nomadic tribes to the mobility of corporate managers, the search for a new geographic location to satisfy the sustenance needs of millions of individuals, families, and whole communities has made mobility a subject of increasing study for anthropologists, geographers, sociologists, planners, and scientists of many other disciplines. Historically, international migration has been the focus of considerable research, but as international movement lessens, internal migration between rural and urban areas takes on greater demographic significance. This demographic significance—how migration affects population growth, the differences in migrant streams, and the impact of migration on other characteristics of individuals and societies—makes the analysis of migration essential to understanding societal transformations.

Before analysis or the modeling of migration, however, must come its measurement. The twin problems of definition and methodology, especially with respect to the measurement of migration, have hindered furtherance of demographic theory. From a demographer's perspective, the measurement of mobility and the role of migration in population change need to be more closely linked with the analysis of natural increase.

The Measurement of Demographic Events

Ryder (1964) has laid out succinctly the elements of the basic population model. First, a population is an aggregate of individuals who are defined according to a space-time frame. Simply put, population is the number of people in some geographic space in a given time period. And the fundamental question concerning a population is how it changes—its growth or decline—over time and in space. This change during a time interval is a result of additions to the population (births and in-migrants) and subtractions from the population (deaths and out-migrants). These four components make up the "demographic equation":

(Population growth)=(Births)−(Deaths)+(In-migrants)−(Out-migrants)

The result of subtracting deaths from births for a specified time interval is called natural increase (or natural decrease, if deaths exceed births) of a population, and the difference between the in-migrants and out-migrants is net migration.

Although demographic events occur to individuals and are microdynamic in that the individual experiences change over time (i.e., one enters the population at birth, ages, and leaves the population at death), these events are also macrodynamic. A population experiences a birthrate, a death rate, and in its temporal existence, its age structure may change as the vital processes interact in a society. When death rates decline and fertility rates remain high, the average age of the population declines. The explanation of this seeming contradiction is that reduced death rates contribute substantially to the survival of young persons. However, when the fertility rate declines, the proportion of young people declines and the population grows older, i.e., the average age increases.

Similarly, as young people migrate to a community, *ceteris paribus,* they increase the proportion of younger persons and lower the average age. As young people migrate from a community without replacement, the consequence is a proportionate increase in older people and an aging of the population. Age is thus the link between an individual's history and the history of a population. Age similarly defines an individual within a cohort. A cohort (defined as all those who experience the same demographic event in a common time interval, such as a birth cohort of 1950 or a marriage cohort of 1975) is the primary demographic grouping of individuals. To the cohorts—the population age-groups at risk to experience an event—occur fertility, mortality, and migration.

The concept of "a population at risk to experience some event" underpins the measurement of vital statistics and migration rates. In the measurement of crude birthrates, the total number of births in a specified area and time interval is divided by the population at risk during that interval. The population at risk is usually an estimate of the midyear population, which represents an average of the number beginning and ending the year. Similarly, a crude death rate is the total number of deaths in a given space and time interval divided by the population at risk to die—the midyear number of people. Multiplying each of these ratios by some constant, such as 1,000, yields a crude birthrate (CBR) or death rate (CDR) per 1,000 population. Refinements of these rates by age, sex, parity, and so forth can be found in Shryock and Siegel (1973).

$$\text{CBR} = \frac{\text{Births}}{\text{Population (midyear)}} \times K \qquad \text{CDR} = \frac{\text{Deaths}}{\text{Population (midyear)}} \times K$$

The measurement of migration is unfortunately not so straightforward. An out-migration rate for a specific geographic area clearly has the possibility of a population at risk to out-migrate for its denominator. An in-migration rate for the same area, however, has as its population at risk the remainder of the country, and, of course, the calculation of net migration is impossible without a common denominator of the same population base. As a practical matter, the population of the area of destination is used for both rates.

$$\text{Out-migration rate} = \frac{\text{Number of out-migrants in interval}}{\text{Population at beginning of interval}} \times K$$

$$\text{In-migration rate} = \frac{\text{Number of in-migrants in interval}}{\text{Population at beginning of interval}} \times K$$

Matras (1973) suggests two variations which provide very useful infor-

6   Internal Migration Systems

Table 1. Origin–Destination Matrix for U.S. Regions, 1970–1975, for Population Age 5 and Over.

1970 Origin	1975 Destination (outflow proportions)					Number
	Northeast	North Central	South	West	Total	in thousands
Northeast	.943	.009	.036	.012	1.00	(41,986)
North Central	.006	.942	.033	.019	1.00	(50,397)
South	.010	.015	.960	.015	1.00	(56,294)
West	.007	.016	.030	.947	1.00	(30,812)

Source: U.S. Bureau of the Census (1975). Excludes those abroad and no report on mobility.

mation to the student of migration. First, an inflow proportion (or in-migration ratio) measures the proportion of population in a destination that in-migrated during the time interval. It is computed thus:

$$\text{Inflow proportion} = \frac{\text{Number of in-migrants}}{\text{Final population at end of interval}}$$

The difference between the inflow and in-migration measures is that the former incorporates the migrants into the denominator using the population at the end of the interval, whereas the latter does not.

A second variation is the outflow rate. When calculated as proportions of the initial population for all destinations, a complete set of out-migration rates forms an outflow table or a mobility matrix. This matrix reveals both origin and destination of migrants and the differential rates among areas. A very simplified but instructive example from the United States shows the origin–destination matrix for interregional migration from 1970 to 1975 (U.S. Bureau of the Census 1975).

The outflow matrix is a useful tool for understanding migration streams and the changing distribution of the population across regional lines. First, reading down the diagonal of Table 1, we see that over 94 percent of the residents in each region remained in the same region. From the Northeast, the largest migration stream was to the South (3.6 percent of those living in the Northeast in 1970 had moved to the South by 1975). Similarly, for the North Central and West regions, the largest out-migration was to the South. The South, on the other hand, showed a high retention rate (96 percent of its original residents were still there, and lower proportions of Southerners migrated to the other regions).

The consequences of a mobility matrix with these sets of outflow rates are shown in Table 2. Over the five-year period, the Northeast and North Central regions lost, on balance, population to the South and West, with

Table 2. *Percentage Distribution of U.S. Population, 5 Years of Age and Over, by Regions, 1970 and 1975.*

Regions	1970	1975
Northeast	23.4	22.6
North Central	28.1	27.4
South	31.3	32.4
West	17.2	17.6
Total	100.0	100.0
(Number)	(179,489,000)	(179,489,000)

Source: U.S. Bureau of the Census (1975); calculations by author.

the South increasing its proportion of the U.S. population from 31.3 percent to 32.4 percent. Although the increase was only 1.1 percent, it meant a net migration of 1.8 million people to the South in a five-year interval.

The value of the mobility analysis in the matrix format is that the process by which one region grows at the others' expense is quantified and provides a model of the change occurring through migration. It is the transition matrix that specifies the process and delineates structural changes. One can then ask, If the migration rates remained the same, what would the distribution of the population be in 1980? By adding to the migration matrix a matrix of fertility and mortality rates, one could produce a complete population projection (Keyfitz 1964; Rogers 1966; Shryock and Siegel 1973).

Data Sources

The methods of measuring migration assume a system of data collection. Such data may not be readily available, and sources of information may need to be developed. The most common source of data on migration is a census or a sample survey of households. A second major source is a population registration system in which individuals must transfer their record or register in the new location when they move. Few developing countries have adequate registration systems for internal migration statistics. Some countries that do are Denmark, Sweden, Belgium, West Germany, Poland, the USSR, Spain, Israel, Japan, and Taiwan. Miscellaneous sources include other national record systems, such as social-security systems and income-tax files, and local data systems, such as utility hookup records or city directories.

Mobility data from a census or survey usually take the form of responses to one or two questions about a person's place of birth or place of

residence one, five, or any given number of years ago. Along the same
lines, duration-of-residence questions tap the interval of time the individual has lived in a community. In some instances, elaborate residence
histories permit the analysis of trends in migration by age cohort and
other characteristics of the individual, as well as characteristics of origin
and destination. (See Taeuber et al., 1968 for an extensive analysis of a
U.S. residential history study.)

Estimating Migration with Incomplete Data

When no migration statistics are formally collected, but vital statistics—
i.e., birth and death records—are adequate, one can determine, using the
balancing equation, estimates of net migration for a given time interval
and geographic area. The balancing or demographic equation was earlier
described; by rearranging the terms, one gets the equation

Net Migration = (Population Growth) − (Natural Increase),

where Population Growth = (Population at time 2) − (Population at time
1), and Natural Increase = (Births) − (Deaths). This method of estimating
net migration is called the vital statistics residual method. However, if
errors occur in vital registration coverage, or if errors occur in the coverage
of census enumeration which determines the population size at the beginning and ending of the interval, all these errors are combined and make
the net migration estimate less accurate. This method and those described
below also assume constant geographic boundaries; that is, if a city grows
by annexation, one must control for this areal redefinition or the estimates
of net migration will be in error. This method also misses the dynamic of
in- and out-migration shown in a mobility matrix, but its data demands
are simpler, and therefore it is often used for internal and international
migration estimation. It may also be used to estimate net migration by
sex, race, or any characteristic which does not change over time.

A second residual method to estimate net migration by age is called the
survival-rate method. The principle involved is elementary; as a cohort
ages, its members die according to a regime of mortality rates. One
estimates the expected number surviving from one time interval to the
next and subtracts the expected number from the known population of
that age. The difference is an estimate of the net migration. The basic
formula is

$$\text{Net Migration}_{(\text{age } X + t)} = \text{Pop}^t_{(\text{age } X + t)} - S\,\text{Pop}^0_{(\text{age } X)}$$

Where X is an age group

t is the interval in years between censuses

Pop_X^0 is the population age X at the first census

Pop_{X+t}^t is the population X + t years later, at the time of the second census

S is the survival rate calculated from a life table, or a census survival rate calculated as a ratio of the same national cohort at successive censuses

This is known as the forward survival rate insofar as one is projecting an expected number by age forward t years to the next age grouping. The reverse survival rate estimates the expected population at the earlier period by dividing thus:

$$\frac{Pop^t \, X + t}{S.}$$

Since these two methods yield slightly different results, it is common to average them for the final migration estimate.

Cohort Analysis of Migration

Prior to a discussion of empirical generalizations concerning migration and as both an introduction to the topic and an example of cohort analysis of migration, an abbreviated table (Table 3) is incorporated from work by Karl Taeuber (1967) in which he analyzes the residential mobility of U.S. farm-born cohorts. The source of data is a survey of residential histories from which Taeuber classifies the native, farm-born population by age and cohort (year of birth) as well as origin and destination. Table 3 is an excellent example for demonstrating intracohort—i.e., within cohort—and intercohort analysis of migration.

The first row of percentages for each age is a retention rate–the percent still on a farm at that age. For each cohort, a metro–nonmetro origin and destination are provided. Taeuber summarizes the results of this table:

1. Intra-cohort comparisons, nonmetropolitan origin (read down nonmetro columns). As the members of each cohort grow older, farm-retention rates decline. In most cohorts there is a substantial off-farm movement by age 18 and continuing until age 34. There is little net change in farm residence from age 34–44, but a resumed loss of farm population during older ages. By age 65 and over, it is likely that fewer

Table 3. *Distribution by Type of Residence at Selected Ages for Cohorts by Metropolitan Location of Birthplace for Native Farm-Born Population, U.S., 1958.*

| | Cohort and location of farm birthplace | | | | | | | |
| | 1933–1940 | | 1923–1933 | | 1913–1923 | | 1903–1913 | |
Type of Residence at selected ages	Non-metro	Metro	Non-metro	Metro	Non-metro	Metro	Non-metro	Metro
At age 18								
Farm	64	76	70	77	74	72	74	73
Nonmetro	20	6	17	4	16	8	15	5
Metro	16	18	13	19	10	20	10	22
At age 24								
Farm	35	45	43	49	55	52	58	54
Nonmetro	36	10	31	13	25	12	23	10
Metro	28	45	26	37	19	36	18	37
At age 34								
Farm			37	36	40	38	47	39
Nonmetro			35	23	32	13	30	13
Metro			28	41	28	48	23	47
At age 44								
Farm					40	38	42	37
Nonmetro					32	24	33	13
Metro					28	38	25	50

Note: Within columns, each set of 3 percentages sums to 100, except for rounding errors.
Source: Taeuber (1967), recalculated by author.

than one-third of the members of any farm-born cohort will still be farm residents.

2. Intra-cohort comparisons, metropolitan origin (read down metro columns). The results are virtually identical to those for persons of nonmetropolitan origin, summarized in (1) above.

3. Inter-cohort comparisons, nonmetropolitan origin (read across columns). Farm-retention rates at age 18 and at each subsequent age are less, the younger the cohort. There has been a change in the timing of off-farm movement, with the younger cohorts displaying greater rates at earlier ages and (probably) lesser rates at older ages relative to those for the older cohorts.

4. Inter-cohort comparisons, metropolitan origin (read across columns). The metropolitan cohorts are more similar one with another in patterns of farm retention than are the non-

metropolitan cohorts. The only substantial trend is a greater rate of off-farm movement at ages 18–24 among the younger cohorts. (1967, p. 26–28.)

Since this material is illustrative, I have not described the destinations of each cohort, whether they moved to a metro or a nonmetro location. In the article, Taeuber elaborates in detail the type of destination—large city, small city, rural area—which provides an insight into the stages U.S. migrants traveled in the rural-to-urban movement. One can quickly see the limitations of cohort data. Young persons have not yet had an opportunity to live out their complete migration experience, resulting in an extremely abbreviated history.

Models of Migration

Various strategies for migration prediction become important as one tries to explain historical patterns of migration and predict future trends. Two generalized models can be described: the macroanalytic models that focus on the place-to-place flows among a system of locations, and the microanalytic models that emphasize the decision to move and the selection of a destination as a result of individual social characteristics, preferences, and behavioral constraints.

Place-to-place theoretical models measure movement between places or whole sectors of society, such as rural–urban, metro–nonmetro, or between regions. Researchers have tried to provide a concise mathematical expression of this process (for example, the P_1P_2/D gravity model of Zipf 1946). Zipf's theory of frictional costs was tested on transportation flows between communities and then applied to migration flows. The gravity model hypothesizes that the migration between place 1 and place 2 is a positive multiplicative result of the size of the population in each place, but inversely related to the distance separating the two places; i.e., the greater the distance and therefore the costs in transportation, communication, etc., the less the interchange of migrants.

Stouffer (1962) later refined this conceptualization by introducing the concept of intervening opportunities and competing migrants as measures of social rather than spatial distance. Galle and Taeuber (1966) have compared the two models and found that the model of intervening opportunities explains intercity migration better than the Zipf gravity model does. Stouffer argued that the volume of migration from one place to another is associated not simply with the number of people in the two places, but with the number of opportunities in each place. Two factors, however, lessen the migration. First, intervening opportunities reduce migration between two points. For example, the migration between Chicago and New Orleans is lessened by opportunities available in St. Louis and all other intervening locations. Second, competing migrants would further lower the volume of migrants between the two places; e.g., in Chicago, the opportunities that attract migrants from closer communities and states would thus lessen the potential New Orleans-to-Chicago stream. By stressing opportunities, Stouffer opened up to migration analysis a wide array of sociological characteristics besides economic opportunities that make a city differentially attractive. Indices of culture, language, religion, and ethnic similarity are useful in understanding both the fact of and lack of migration (Heide 1963).

The weakness of the place-to-place models is their inability to answer questions about total in- and out-migration or about migration by age, sex, race, or any differential characteristics of migrants.

Conceptually, recent migration research has moved away from the gravity or intervening-opportunities model and focused on total levels of in- and out-migration in a two-area context: a particular place and the remainder of the total areal unit, such as a metropolitan area and the rest of a country. Lowry (1966) presented some brief illustrative data to show that in-migration to a U.S. metropolitan area from all other areas is a function of the character and condition of the destination's labor market, whereas out-migration is a function of the size and age-sex composition of the population resident in the area. Lansing and Mueller (1967), in their research on the determinants of geographic mobility, found a quite similar result; low levels of employment opportunities or low income levels in an area did not stimulate out-migration, but high levels of employment opportunities attracted in-migration.

These asymmetrical influences of community characteristics upon in- and out-migration mean that an appropriate way to simplify migration data would be to decompose the net migration statistic into its two components. Then, the dependent variable would be the volume of in-migration to one place from all other places, and the variables associated with this movement could be determined. Similarly, the out-migration from a given place could be determined, with a specified set of variables affecting this movement. Finally, the difference between these two streams would yield either a positive or a negative net population change due to migration. (See Zuiches 1970 for an example of such an analysis, using U.S. nonmetropolitan cities.)

An excellent synthesis of the macroanalytic models is given in Lee's 1966 paper, "A Theory of Migration." Defining migration broadly as a "permanent or semi-permanent change of residence," he then outlines the factors involved in the act of migration:

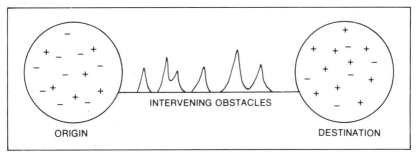

Figure 1. Origin and Destination Factors and Intervening Obstacles in Migration: "The Push-Pull Obstacles" Model.
Source: Lee, 1966.

1. Factors associated with area of origin
2. Factors associated with area of destination
3. Intervening obstacles
4. Personal factors

For every mover, the origin will possess positive and negative factors, as will the destination, and a set of intervening obstacles must be overcome to complete the move. Theoretically, individuals weigh all in a complex set of calculations and are either pushed by the severe negative factors out of a place of origin or attracted by the positive attributes to another place. In addition, Lee introduces the characteristics of the migrant. Migrant differentials have long been noted (Davis 1974; Lansing and Mueller 1967; Ravenstein 1885, 1889; Taeuber et al. 1968). Migration is selective, especially of the young. But most studies have shown it is also selective of the better educated, the higher occupational classes, and the youth of a community, and males when long distances are involved. Those who could contribute most to a place of origin most often leave.

Since migration is both a societal and an individual adaptive mechanism to technological, sustenance, cultural, and economic opportunities, the costs are thus borne by one segment of a society and the benefits accrue to others. Who benefits and how policies might be adopted to share equitably the burdens of migration and congested urban destinations are issues developing societies must face. Turner (1976) has suggested a range of fundamental policies for dealing with pressures of rural-to-urban migration, such as (a) slowing overall population growth, (b) supporting small cities as potential destinations, (c) adopting a set of tax incentives and disincentives to channel mobility, (d) adopting authoritarian measures (e.g., the internal passport), and (e) planning for overall societal transformation that meets the needs of the people. Such structural policies are appropriate for consideration in macroanalytic migration work.

The level of microanalytic models addresses the behavioral, rather than structural, dynamics of mobility decisions. The earlier work of Taeuber on residential histories demonstrated the gap in migration analysis, i.e., an understanding of the decision-making process to predict future mobility. Lansing and Mueller (1967) noted that the decision to move required a strong attractive force more than a strong "push" factor. Individuals seem to have an inherent inertia. Work by Morrison (1967) has clearly shown that duration of residence affects the propensity to move. The longer one stays in a location, the less likely one is to move. Conversely, the more often one moves, the more likely one will be a "chronic mover" (Morrison 1971). Finally, Morrison (1973) has argued that three factors affect one's threshold of mobility: (a) stage in the life cycle, (b) occupational constraints, and (c) prior migration experience. Each of these individual attributes contributes to the migration decision. (See Speare 1970 for a rough test of this model.)

Approaching the issue from a different perspective are the demographers and community researchers who have tried to estimate migration and future population trends by interviewing, through sample surveys, individuals about their community ideals, satisfaction, and preferences (Dillman 1973; Fuguitt and Zuiches 1975). The preference researchers argue that preferences and mobility plans and expectations are indicative of future migration patterns. A comparable stream of research in geography uses "mental maps" as a technique for measuring awareness and preferences (Fuller and Chapman 1974); the application of such maps to migration research is readily apparent.

Next Steps in Migration Research

This chapter is not the place to outline efforts which integrate structural and individual models of migration, but recent efforts could be noted. Morrison (1973) has suggested a conjunctive framework for migration analysis in which first, individual decisions about moving or staying operate, and then, individuals are allocated according to the macroanalytic models earlier described. Others (Patrick and Ritchey 1974; Richmond 1969; Zelinsky 1971) have considered the process of societal transformation from agricultural to industrial, from rural- to urban-dominated, from traditional *Gemeinschaft* to a highly organized division of labor and complex social structure. In each of these transformations, the relationship between societal development and population, and especially migration, is a key theoretical issue. The following chapters will provide applications of migration theory to developing countries in Asia, Africa, and Latin America.

References

* Michigan Agricultural Experiment Station Journal Article No. 7910
Beale, Calvin L. 1975. "The Revival of Population Growth in Nonmetropolitan America." Washington, D.C.: Economic Research Service, U.S. Department of Agriculture, ERS-605.
Davis, Kingsley. 1974. "The Migrations of Human Populations." Chap. 5 in *The Human Population*. San Francisco: W. H. Freeman.
Dillman, Don A. 1973. "Population Distribution Policy and People's Attitudes—Current Knowledge and Needed Research." Washington, D.C.: Urban Land Institute, with a grant from U.S. Department of Housing and Urban Development.
Fuguitt, Glenn V. and James J. Zuiches. 1975. "Residential Preferences and Population Distribution," *Demography*, 12: 491–504.
Fuller, Gary and Murray Chapman. 1974. "On the Role of Mental Maps in Migration Research," *International Migration Review*, 8: 491–506.
Galle, Omer R. and Karl E. Taeuber. 1966. "Metropolitan Migration and Intervening Opportunities," *American Sociological Review*, 31: 5–13.
Heide, H. ter. 1963. "Migration Models and Their Significance for Population Forecasts," *Milbank Memorial Fund Quarterly*, 41: 56–76.
Keyfitz, Nathan. 1964. "Matrix Multiplication as a Technique of Population Analysis," *Milbank Memorial Fund Quarterly*, 42: 68–84.
Lansing, J. B. and Eva Mueller. 1967. *The Geographic Mobility of Labor*. Ann Arbor, Mich.: University of Michigan Survey Research Center, Institute for Social Research.
Lee, Everett S. 1966. "A Theory of Migration," *Demography*, 3: 47–57.
Lowry, Ira S. 1966. *Migration and Metropolitan Growth: Two Analytical Models*. San Francisco: Chandler.
Matras, Judah. 1973. *Populations and Societies*. Englewood Cliffs, N.J.: Prentice-Hall.
Morrison, Peter A. 1967. "Duration of Residence and Prospective Migration: The Evaluation of a Stochastic Model," *Demography*, 4: 553–61.
Morrison, Peter A. 1971. "Chronic Movers and the Future Redistribution of Population," *Demography*, 8: 171–84.
Morrison, Peter A. 1973. "Theoretical Issues in the Design of Population Mobility Models," *Environment and Behavior*, 5: 125–34.
Patrick, Clifford H. and P. Neal Ritchey. 1974. "Changes in Population and Employment as Processes in Regional Development," *Rural Sociology*, 39: 224–37.
Ravenstein, E. G. 1885. "The Laws of Migration," Part I. *Journal of the Royal Statistical Society*, 48: 167–227.

Ravenstein, E. G. 1889. "The Laws of Migration," Part II. *Journal of the Royal Statistical Society,* 52: 241–301.

Richmond, Anthony H. 1969. "Sociology of Migration in Industrial and Post-Industrial Societies," Chap. 9 in *Migration,* J. A. Jackson (ed.), Cambridge: Cambridge University Press.

Rogers, Andrei. 1966. "Matrix Methods of Population Analysis," *Journal of the American Institute of Planners,* 32: 40–44.

Ryder, Norman B. 1964. "Notes on the Concept of a Population," *American Journal of Sociology,* 69: 447–63.

Speare, Alden. 1970. "Home Ownership, Life Cycle Stage, and Residential Mobility," *Demography,* 7: 449–58.

Shryock, Henry S. and Jacob Siegel. 1973. *The Methods and Materials of Demography,* Vols. I and II. Washington, D.C.: U.S. Government Printing Office.

Stouffer, Samuel A. 1962. *Social Research to Test Ideas.* New York: The Free Press of Glencoe.

Taeuber, Karl E. 1967. "The Residential Redistribution of Farm-born Cohorts," *Rural Sociology,* 32: 20–36.

Taeuber, K. E., L. Chiazze, Jr. and William Haenszel. 1968. *Migration in the United States.* Washington, D.C.: U.S. Government Printing Office.

Turner, Frederick C. 1976. "The Rush to the Cities in Latin America," *Science,* 192: 955–62.

U. S. Bureau of the Census. 1975. "Mobility of the Population of the United States: March, 1970 to 1975," *Current Population Reports,* Series P-20, No. 285. Washington, D.C.: U.S. Government Printing Office.

Zelinsky, Wilbur. 1971. "The Hypothesis of the Mobility Transition," *The Geographical Review,* 61: 219–49.

Zipf, George K. 1946. "The P_1P_2/D Hypothesis: On the Intercity Movement of Persons," *American Sociological Review,* 11: 677–86.

Zuiches, James J. 1970. "In-migration and Growth of Nonmetropolitan Urban Places," *Rural Sociology,* 35: 410–20.

Ernst C. Griffin and
Lynden S. Williams

Social Implications of Changing Population Patterns: The Case of Rural Depopulation in Colombia

Scholars concerned with demographic patterns in Latin America have focused attention on rapid total population growth and the explosive surge in the size of cities. Such attention is merited. Annual national growth rates of 3 percent and urban growth rates in excess of 5 percent have been common during the past two decades. In Colombia, for example, the population nearly doubled between 1951 and 1973, increasing from 11. 5 million to over 21 million.[1]

Within this setting, the topic of rural depopulation might seem incongruous. Indeed, when considering population growth and change in Latin America, it has been customary to emphasize that despite high rates of internal migration from rural to urban areas, absolute increases have continued to occur among rural populations. It is widely assumed, and often stated, that rural depopulation is prevented in Latin America by extraordinarily high rates of natural population increase in rural areas.[2] *But this generalization is no longer valid in Colombia.* Comparisons of census data for 1951 through 1973 indicate that there has been an absolute loss in rural population, especially within the traditional core areas of the country. Rural depopulation has begun on a massive scale and is accelerating.[3] The purpose of this chapter is to describe the process of rural depopulation in Colombia and to analyze some of its causes and consequences.

Data and Methodology

The study area for this research includes all of Colombia that had departmental status in 1973. The *intendencias* and *comisarías*, territories lacking departmental status which comprise roughly the eastern half of the country, are excluded from the study because no data were available. These territories contained less than 3 percent of the total Colombian population in 1973 and are mainly pioneer zones.

Changes in total population were compared by *municipios* for the three census periods 1938–1951, 1951–1964, and 1964–1973.[4] (During these three census periods, the statistical definition of an urban area remained unchanged: an agglomerated population center of 1,500 or more which provided urban functions. Therefore, rural depopulation cannot be the result of redefinition of terms.) The number of *municipios* and their areal extent are changed frequently in Colombia. To compensate for such changes, the 1973 census data were aggregated to 1964 *municipio* boundaries and the 1964 data to 1951 boundaries so that comparability of data collection units could be maintained. This process allows changes to be measured between spatial entities over time.

Indices of Change

Colombia has been experiencing a radical change in the relationship between urban and rural population since the 1940s.[5] In 1938, less than 31 percent of the country's population was considered urban. By 1973, an estimated 61 percent lived in urban areas. Occurring during a time of rapid total population growth, that percentage increase represents a fivefold absolute increase in urban population (from 2.7 to nearly 13 million). This same process is taking place in nearly all Latin American countries and of itself is not particularly noteworthy. Indeed, the concept of Latin America as a predominantly rural, largely traditional agrarian region is outdated. The population explosion in Colombia has occurred primarily in urban areas. The continued agglomeration of inhabitants in major urban centers reinforces and exaggerates one of the principal demographic features of Latin America, a highly clustered population.[6]

While the nation's urban population has soared since 1938, rural population has also increased in absolute terms. Between 1938 and 1951, the rural sector grew by slightly over one million (roughly from 6 to 7 million), which represented more than a third of total national growth. During the 1951–1964 period, rural areas added another 1.3 million people, at a rate slightly less than that of the previous intercensal period, despite the fact that the national population growth rate jumped a full percentage point.

More significantly, though, Colombia's rural population decreased by 168,000 (from 8.39 to 8.22 million), or 2 percent, between 1964 and 1973. This decrease in rural population took place most notably in the densely settled highland, rural areas of the nation: Boyacá, Antióquia, Viejo Caldas, Tolima, and Nariño. This may portend a general process occurring (or about to occur) in other Latin American countries. Only under exceptional conditions has rural depopulation been reported elsewhere in the region, and then only with respect to limited areas.[7]

Although the rural growth rate of Colombia during the latest intercensal period suggests a demographically stagnant region, one with high death rates and low birthrates, this is emphatically not the case. Age-specific birthrates and death rates of rural Colombia are consistent with extremely rapid population growth. The massive out-migration of young people from rural areas has lowered birthrates, increased death rates, and reduced population in absolute terms. Those who suggest that the urban explosion in Latin America is primarily the result of population growth per se, rather than rural-to-urban migration, miss the crucial point that migration produces an age structure tending toward population growth in the urban receiving centers and toward reducing growth in the areas of out-migration.

Changes in Total Population

Rural population loss is not new to Colombia. During the late 1940s and continuing into the 1950s, many *municipios,* particularly in Tolima, Huila, and parts of Boyacá, lost inhabitants in absolute terms. Such losses were due to *La Violencia,* a chaotic period of internecine struggle between Liberal and Conservative political factors in which as many as 250,000 people may have been killed in rural areas.[8] By computing changes in total population (urban and rural) for the 1951–1964 intercensal period, one can show that significant numbers of *municipios*—nearly 20 percent of the nation's total—lost population. However, many of these *municipios* were found to be in areas not normally associated with the political and social upheavals of *La Violencia.*

In order to verify this trend, total population change by *municipio* was computed for the 1964–1973 census period. Of 857 *municipios,* 392 or 45 percent had lost population in absolute terms. Of these, 302 *municipios* had lost more than 5 percent and 208 *municipios* had lost more than 10 percent of their 1964 total population.

It is apparent, then, that a process first identifiable for the decade of the 1950s accelerated during the 1960s. Given an estimated increase in total population for the nation of over 20 percent during the 1964–1973 intercensal period, it is obvious that substantial increases occurred within specific parts of the country, and that the bulk of it took place in urban centers. This particularly true for Bogotá, which grew by 1.1 million to over 2.8 million in 1973, while Medellín, the country's second city, increased by almost half a million to reach 1.1 million, and Cali added a quarter-million people and now has about 900,000 in population. These cities alone account for nearly one-half of the nation's total population increase. With cities expanding more rapidly than populations in general, it is evident that noncity areas were being depopulated. Furthermore, if such losses can be identified on the basis of total population change, depopulation must be an even more significant process in rural areas where rural-to-urban migration rates are extremely high.

Changes in Rural Population

To verify rural depopulation, it was necessary to disaggregate total population into rural and urban components. On this basis, nearly 60 percent of all Colombian *municipios* (511 of 857) lost rural population in absolute terms between 1964 and 1973. Two-thirds of these lost more than 10 percent of their 1964 rural population. The great mass of *municipios* losing people were located in the densely populated traditional core areas of Colombian settlement: the eastern Cordillera, Antióquia, and Nariño. The majority of the *municipios* which lost rural population in the 1951–1964 period continued to lose population after 1964 as well.

Although most of the *municipios* losing population were in the historical settlement nodes of the country, many *municipios* in what are normally described as dynamic frontier or colonization zones lost people in absolute terms. *Municipios* in parts of the Llanos, such as Meta, and the middle Magdalena Valley which showed population gains during the 1950s and early 1960s now appear to be losing people.[9]

Causes Of Rural Depopulation

Rural depopulation is an obvious concomitant of rapid and continued urbanization, as is well evidenced by the technologically advanced countries of the world. But in a country such as Colombia, with average annual growth rates hovering near 3 percent during the last three decades and high fertility levels in rural areas, absolute population losses in the countryside might seem unlikely.[10] However, a number of factors combine to encourage ever-increasing numbers of people to abandon rural areas, including the initial impetus of *La Violencia,* a lack of adequate social services, underemployment and unemployment, few job opportunities outside of agriculture, the absence of meaningful agrarian reform, and government policies which favor spending and focus attention on urban development.

Colombia is archetypical of Latin America in terms of internal migration.[11] The unending parade of migrants bound for urban centers began during the early 1930s as a result of the initial onslaught of violence.

Sporadic bouts of sectarian violence began in many small towns and spilled over into rural areas as the first legal transition between Colombia's two major political parties began to take place. These disorders, the precursors of *La Violencia,* encouraged many people to abandon the countryside for the safety of the towns and cities. Bogotá and Medellín were the primary foci of these earliest migrants, but Cali, Barranquilla, and a myriad of secondary and tertiary centers were to become important in following decades. If nothing else, these first urban-bound migrants of the 1930s made traditional rural people aware of the potentials of leaving the countryside and established some of the early kinship communication networks between city dwellers and rural peasants.

La Violencia burst forth in earnest in 1948 with the assassination of Jorge Eliécer Gaitán, the revered Liberal populist. Though the initial reaction, especially the *Bogotazo,* was felt primarily in urban areas, *La Violencia* soon settled down to become a macabre, rural-oriented blood-bath which lasted more than a decade and left perhaps a quarter-million dead. During the period 1948–1958, huge numbers of people fled from the scenes of most severe struggle. Tolima, Huila, portions of Boyacá and Antióquia were especially noted as the stages upon which *La Violencia*'s ugly passion play unfolded. Under such circumstances, rural depopulation not only seems reasonable but could be anticipated as sane behavior.

Although *La Violencia* was widespread geographically, its occurrence over a number of years cannot be used to "explain" the recent massive rates of rural-to-urban migration. Perhaps the most important impact of *La Violencia* was to uproot large numbers of people who previously had been place-specific and to weaken the traditional ties binding peasants to their rural birthplaces. In this case, *La Violencia* might be likened to the Mexican Revolution as a vehicle for creating physical and, ultimately, social mobility.

Other socioeconomic conditions can provide a better understanding of internal migration stimuli in Colombia during the past fifteen years. Even today, much of the rural area of the nation lacks the most basic social services. Gains are being made in electrification, but most of the country-side still lacks electricity. Rural schools are increasing in numbers, but their quality remains low, and there are not sufficient spaces for all school-aged children or teachers to teach them. Despite government efforts to improve health care in the countryside, few doctors are available to rural peasants, and rural clinics and hospitals are few. Government programs such as minimum-wage laws go unenforced, thus not only creating economic hardships for peasants and their families, but also exaggerating the existing perception of great economic distinctions between urban places and the countryside.

Rapid growth over several decades within the densely populated rural settlement cores of the country has increased pressures on the limited agricultural land base and existing employment structures. Agriculture dominates the countryside, and there are few alternate employment opportunities. These conditions are magnified by a severe *latifundio-minifundio* (i.e., estate size) dichotomy. Despite a detailed agrarian reform law which provides for expropriation of underutilized lands, the Colombian government has not pursued large-scale land redistribution programs. It has chosen instead to concentrate on colonization and resettlement projects, mainly in lowland frontier areas. This approach has been unsuccessful in meeting the country's pressing social need for meaningful agrarian reform. Increasing mechanization on large farms further complicates the problem. As a result, underemployment and unemployment force peasants out of the countryside and into the cities.

While these "push" forces are felt in rural areas of Colombia, the social and economic attractiveness of the nation's cities has continued to improve. In fact, most global government policies which have been implemented enhance the modernity of the urban centers, while at the same time they heighten the contrasts with the traditions of the countryside. The major cornerstones of development over the last decade have stressed urban construction, increased industrialization, and stimulation of growth in intermediate-sized cities. These have given rise to unprecedented building booms in the major cities which have not only drastically altered skylines, but have also created large numbers of unskilled construction jobs attractive to migrants. Increased emphasis on expanding industry has had a similar effect, especially in Medellín, Cali, and Barranquilla. And the added attention paid to intermediate-sized cities with populations from 100,000 to 250,000 has created increased social and economic opportunity in such places. Increasingly, greater amounts of capital are poured into the cities to provide basic services such as streets, housing, electricity, water, sewerage, schools, and hospitals for the massive influx of newcomers and to make up for existing deficits in these services. Such expenditures often are made to the exclusion of improvements in rural areas. In Colombia, at least, the flood of migrants to the cities is as much or more a result of the perceived socioeconomic attractiveness of urban centers as it is of long-standing deficiencies within the rural areas.

Implications

As Colombia has entered this stage of rural depopulation, a number of possibilities present themselves. Most important, widespread urbanization and declining rural populations are conditions which presage rapid changes in fertility. It would seem logical to expect a radical decrease in fertility levels for the nation over a relatively short period of time as traditional attitudes toward children and their social and economic roles change. Additionally, young people migrate in disproportionately large numbers. This leaves rural areas with an older-than-normal population and drains some of the better-educated peasantry from the land. It also removes from the countryside a significant part of the female population just entering the childbearing years. Women are more likely than men to migrate to urban places; this not only lessens the number of females in rural areas, but transfers them to cities where they are likely to marry at a somewhat later age and have fewer live births than their peasant counterparts. Low-paying jobs as domestics, the most numerous employment opportunities in cities, are available in almost endless quantities. Sex ratios in Bogotá—approximately 80 males per 100 females—reflect the degree to which sex-selective migration is occurring.

Another cause of concern within rural areas has been socioeconomic problems such as lack of jobs, low incomes, and inability to obtain land. Although these problems will not be solved by rural depopulation, to a degree they may be ameliorated. For example, migrants to urban centers frequently send part of their income to relatives who remain in the countryside. Such transfers of income could be significant in improving gross income levels among the rural poor, but little is known as to the extent or impact of such economic transactions in Colombia. In theory at least, fewer people will be competing for the scarce land resources and jobs which are available. Some enlargement of agricultural plots may be possible, more ready access to land might become a possibility for some landless peasants, and rural incomes might rise as surplus labor disappears.

However, many Colombians argue that the conscious efforts of the national government to improve urban centers is a planned oligarchic endeavor to draw people from the rural areas, as a defense against agrarian reform. Land expropriation and redistribution would seriously affect not only income levels, but also the social foundations of the country's ruling elites. Rather than diminishing social contrasts, decreased rural populations will probably result in greater mechanization on large holdings, thus increasing existing inequalities in production between large and small holders, while at the same time displacing labor. Land which does become available for sale as a consequence of migration can most easily be purchased by the wealthier landowners, further increasing inequities in land-tenure patterns and income distributions. Additionally, massive urban populations provide a supply of low-cost labor for construction and industry as well as a ready market for industrial goods supplied by the nation's capitalists in the cities. Both of these conditions favor the oligarchy.

Increased urbanization is accompanied by a series of sociocultural impacts, such as the explosion of urban peripheral slums and shantytowns, underemployment and unemployment, abandonment of unwanted children, lack of adequate public services, and other products of modernization, which are well known and a source of severe sociopolitical stress in Colombia. As the percent of the total population living in urban areas increases, the problems it spawns and nourishes will be magnified. The massing of the poor in urban centers makes them a visible, obvious, undeniable source of need which cannot be ignored. Growing class contradictions will have to be dealt with under such circumstances, or the present political system will not be able to maintain itself without increasing levels of repression.

In conclusion, then, what is taking place in Colombia is rural depopulation on a massive scale. This process has not been reported elsewhere in Latin America on a national basis, yet it is one which argues for significant changes in a variety of sociocultural characteristics within Colombia's countryside as well as its cities. Indeed, it is a logical extension of the social and economic forces set into motion by the modernization of a traditional society.

Notes

1. All of the data cited were taken from the *Censo de Población de Colombia* (1938), the *Censo de Población de Colombia* (Mayo 9 de 1951), the *XIII Censo Nacional de Población* (Julio 15 de 1964), and the *XIV Censo Nacional de Población Y III de Vivienda* (*Resultados Provisionales*) in the *Boletín Mensual de Estadísticas*, No. 279 (Octubre 1974), which are publications of the Departmento Administrativo Nacional de Estadística, Bogotá.

2. Haney, quoting the director of the Colombian Agrarian Reform Institute, stated that rural population growth continues at the rate of about 1,000 farm families per week in spite of rural–urban migration. Emil B. Haney, Jr., "The Minifundia Dilemma: A Colombian Case Study," in *Population Policies and Growth in Latin America*, David Chaplin, ed. (Lexington, Mass.: Lexington Books, 1971). In his widely referenced article on urbanization, Kingsley Davis stated that the rate of out-migration from rural areas in developing countries is not sufficient to offset natural population increase. Kingsley Davis, "The Urbanization of the Human Population," *Scientific American*, 213, no. 3 (September 1965): 51. Also see Harley Browning, "The Demography of the City," in *The Urban Explosion in Latin America*, Glenn Beyer, ed. (Ithaca, N.Y.: Cornell University Press, 1967); John Durand and Cesar Palaez, "Patterns of Urbanization in Latin America," in *The City in Newly Developing Countries*, Gerald Breese, ed., (Englewood Cliffs, N.J.: Prentice-Hall, 1969); Lowdon Wingo, "Latin

American Urbanization: Plan or Process," in *Shaping an Urban Future*, B. Frieden and W. Nash, eds. (Cambridge, Mass.: MIT Press, 1969); and Alan Gilbert, *Latin American Development: A Geographical Perspective*, (Middlesex: Penguin Books, 1974).

3. The process of small-town and rural depopulation is covered in Lynden S. Williams and Ernst C. Griffin, "Rural and Small Town Depopulation in Colombia," *Geographical Review*, 67, no. 1 (January 1978).
4. *Municipios* are the smallest political administrative units of Colombia and are roughly equivalent to counties in the United States.
5. Urban population in Colombia is defined as settlements of 1,500 inhabitants or more with urban functions. In this study, *cabecera* populations are used as a surrogate for urban population and *restos* (non-*cabecera*) are considered rural. *Cabeceras* are the administrative centers of *municipios* and some of these do not have populations of 1,500. On the other hand, some non-*cabeceras* have more than 1,500 persons. The differences introduced when using *cabecera* population totals rather than urban totals are not considered to be significant.
6. Preston E. James, *Latin America*, 4th ed. (New York: Odyssey, 1969), pp. 4–7.
7. For example, see David A. Preston, "Rural Emigration in Andean America," *Human Organization*, 23 (Winter 1969), and R. W. Wilkie, "On the Theory of Process in Human Geography: A Case Study of Migration in Rural Argentina" (Ph.D. dissertation, University of Washington, 1968).
8. Perhaps the best description of this period is German Guzman Campos, *La Violencia en Colombia* (Cali: Ediciones Progreso, 1968).
9. In the case of the lower and middle Magdalena Valley, underenumeration may be responsible for the absolute declines which appear.
10. Insights into Colombia's fertility patterns can be found in Mario Jaramillo Gomez and Robert B. Hartford, *Regulación de la Fecundidad: Conocimientos, Actitudes y Prácticas de la Población Colombiana* (Bogotá: Asociación Colombiana de Facultades de Medicina, División de Estudios de Población, 1968).
11. See Ramiro Cardena, ed, *Las Migraciones Internas* (Bogotá, Asociación Colombiana de Facultades de Medicina, División de Estudios de Población, 1972).

Richard C. Jones

Behavioral Causes and Consequences of Rural–Urban Migration: Special Reference to Venezuela

Rural–Urban Migration

Growth of urban areas in Latin America has roots which are both older than and by nature different from those which nurtured the industrial/urban revolutions of the West. These roots are largely administrative and aesthetic rather than economic, and one can only interpret current demographic movements in Latin America in terms of these roots. The sixteenth-century leaders Charles V and Philip II were not content to enrich Spain; they desired to transplant Spanish life to the New World. The Mediterranean grid-pattern town, with its spacious central plaza flanked by ostentatious administrative structures, became the ideal. In the mind's eye, this plaza became the city, and as such it represented a place of architectural beauty and calm. Aesthetics aside, the cities had important administrative functions, and these were recognized by the Crown. Religious indoctrination and governmental control and "discipline" were facilitated by concentrating ecclesiastical and civil authorities in the cities (Gakenheimer 1967). In fact, the Inca and Aztec empires had already provided the political bases for the functional hierarchy which was subsequently superimposed upon them. The Crown therefore granted indigenous cities to conquerors, both to reward their efforts and to direct the future evolution of the region into a re-created Spain.

Economic motives were also present, of course. Cities were located at mining sites and as commercial entrepôts on the coasts. These cities nevertheless usually coincided with already extant population clusters, and in no case could their formation be considered a response to a process of industrialization. As a result of the grand scheme of Spanish urbanization, sixteen of the twenty largest cities in the Latin America of today were already established by the year 1580.

This historical process has had a major impact on current demographic mobility within Latin American countries. Primate cities had an early start compared with other cities, and as a result, their urban economies and cultural magnetism were accentuated. Actually, there is little in these urban economies today which serves to differentiate Latin America primate cities from primate cities in the developed countries. However, at least two additional ingredients have been added in the case of Latin American primate cities which makes their attractiveness more pronounced. The first of these is what has been called social dualism: the emergence and perpetuation of a dichotomy in social and cultural values between rural and urban areas. The emergence of this dichotomy is frequently found in the customary differences between urban and rural (or industrial and nonindustrial) areas; the dichotomy is subsequently intensified within each area by the attribution to that area of virtues which are responsible for its position (e.g., hard work on one hand, culture and morality on the other). Whether true or not, the attribution of these virtues becomes self-fulfilling over time. As a result, persons with an orientation to urban material values leave rural areas for urban ones. The converse flow occurs much less frequently; but the stronger the dichotomy, the greater the tendency for rural–urban moves.

This brings us to the second ingredient, the phenomenal degree to which Latin American primate cities are the "windows to the world" for their respective countries. Great numbers of people move into the major cities of Latin America for the same reasons that large groups of people gather around a TV set in a shop window in a large Latin American city or a group of rural peasants on a lunch break gather around a radio to listen to a soccer match. They come because they want to know what is going on in the world outside of their limited existence. Frequently the world outside as viewed through the media is distorted; but once "hooked" on the city, few ever return to the countryside, even though their aspirations are not fulfilled in the urban area. If the change from a rural value system to an urban one is common, the reverse is less common; that is, the rural–urban migration pattern is both predominant and essentially irreversible. Thus, the two factors mentioned—social dualism between rural and urban areas and the emanation of information from the cities—are responsible for an *urban world view.*

Two examples of this urban world view illustrate its nature and pervasiveness in Latin America. For the Brazilian federal district of Brasília, Eugene Wilkening (1968) has documented attitudes of urban residents toward rural life which are less than bucolic. Asked to respond to the statement "Farm workers are bad characters," no fewer than 79 percent of the urban interviewees agreed; asked to respond to "People who work in agriculture are more intelligent than those who work in the city," only 13 percent of the urban respondents agreed. Wilkening went a step further, asking residents of rural Brasília how they felt; 83 percent disagreed with the first statement, while 34 percent agreed with the second statement. The two samples agreed on very few attitudinal scales, in fact, despite the fact that they had lifetime migration profiles by origin which were quite similar. One scale on which they did agree (55 percent for both samples) was "No one gives much value to those who work the land."

In another study, Ruben Reina (1964) provides us with fascinating evidence that the urban world view need not be confined to residents of cities. The inhabitants of Flores, Petén, Guatemala, exhibit both a finely honed awareness of national events and a level of social sophistication (costume balls, café societies, civic organizations) expected only of larger cities. Reina explains that in a situation of "environment largely dominated by the forces of nature," the few numbers of the commercial and political elite may try to create a more familiar environment in which "the ideal of living in a 'city' and being urban [becomes] the core of their general cultural orientation." We are indebted to Reina for providing an example of a general reality in Latin America: Urban orientation of the upper classes, as well as of the middle classes which emulate them, is a function of Spanish cultural heritage, and it is a potent force which permeates the most isolated corners of the national space.

The urban world view alone is too vague a concept on which to base a sound explanation of interregional migration. It gives us an idea of why rural–urban migration is so pronounced, but it cannot explain why some cities are more attractive than others. It also ignores recent waves of migration to the "innovative peripheries" (Friedmann 1966, chapter 10) and the existence of important economically attractive forces. Nor does it hint whether the migration it induces has a favorable or an unfavorable impact regionally and nationally. Further investigation is necessary.

Causes of Rural–Urban Migration: Emigration from the Rural Andes

When viewing aggregate interview data, one is impressed with the seeming complexities of migration decisions. Migrants appear to follow rather elaborate migration paths to large urban areas, and the reasons for their moves (as gleaned from surveys) include a gamut of social, environmental, cultural, and economic motives. The complexity of motives may be due to the complexity of questionnaire design and to the tendency for migrants to rationalize a move already made by attributing to it a variety of acceptable motives, ignoring, or having forgotten, the original motives. For the individual migrant the actual migration decision is more straightforward and deterministic. Often no decision is made on the part of dependents at all. For heads of households, at a given moment in time, the decision is made on the basis of the situation at the origin and, usually, the situation at a specific destination where opportunity of a specific sort is known to exist. The difference between perceived net benefits at the origin and at the destination reaches some threshold, and the move is made. This threshold varies with each individual family, but the factors which influence the decision are similar. For conceptual convenience in the current analysis, consider (a) factors which promote emigration from the origin (the rural Andes), (b) factors which promote in-migration to the destination (urban centers), and (c) factors in the resource peripheries which promote in-migration.

Origin Characteristics

The major reason for out-migration from the Andes is land shortage. Land has not only productive importance, but also social importance, and ownership is a chief status symbol in Andean society. For Ecuador, Cisneros (1959) has documented the willingness of highland natives, working under the *huasipunga* system, to migrate seasonally many miles into the tropical lowlands just to work a few acres of their own land. Preston's work in southern Ecuador (1974) reveals the problem of *minifundia,* resulting from increased subdivision of a family's land, which has resulted in seasonal migration to the sugar estates in the west. For Colombia, Dale Adams (1969) cites several rural "push" factors including the dual migration stream to urban centers and to the Llanos Orientales. He cites the monopoly of land by absentee owners, the lack of social opportunities, and rural violence (also see Flinn 1966). In Bolivia, land shortage in the Cochabamba valley was mentioned by potential out-migrants as the most consistent problem they faced in the highlands (Sariola 1960). Finally, research in Huaylas, Peru, points up a static land base as the chief factor in emigration to Lima and Chimbote (Bradfield 1973).

Reasons cited by rural Andean persons for their displeasure with the home area are usually traced to land shortage. For example, Cisneros (1959) lists the three factors found to influence seasonal migration to the Ecuadorian lowlands as (a) economic—greater ease in getting land via the *huasipunga* system; (b) demographic—less population pressure on available land; and (c) political—availability of government land concessions. The major exception to this rule in Latin America is the desire to educate one's children, a desire which siphons away many of the better-off rural families who would otherwise remain in the rural zones.

Destination Characteristics

Objective opportunities at urban destinations have been analyzed in detail by several authors (e.g., Sahota 1968; Schultz 1971; Levy and Wadycki

1972a, 1972b; Carvajal and Geithman 1974). Detailed discussion will not occupy us here. Findings indicate that economic factors (income, unemployment rates), social factors (especially educational levels), and distance are most critical.

Since there has been little systematic study of urban–rural and rural–urban migration, the investigation of these phenomena demands more of our attention. Studies of such moves identify objective destination benefits from both the individual and the regional points of view. Individuals who move into resource frontiers tend to do so in response to strong economic incentives. Flinn and Cartano (1970) found that 51 percent of migrants to Granada, an agricultural town of 3,000 population in the eastern interior of Colombia, came for economic reasons, including 20 percent who moved "to find cheaper or better life" and 14 percent "to find land." Though not Andean, Wilkening's work on Brazil (1968) is relevant because it compares motives for migration into both urban and rural areas in a resource frontier zone (the federal district of Brasília). Job and economic opportunities were listed as most important for 64 percent of in-migrants to rural Brasília, but for only 44 percent of the in-migrants to urban Brasília. Work by the author (Jones and Zannaras 1972) in the state of Portuguesa, Venezuela, indicates that economic motives account for 80 percent of the migration to Turén, an agricultural colony of 9,300 population in 1970, but for only 40 percent of the migration to Acariqua, the regional growth center of the Western Llanos (population 66,000). Finally, Sariola's previously cited study (1960) of the Cochabamba-Santa Cruz migration stream in Bolivia found the greatest preference differentials in favor of Santa Cruz (over the Cochabamba Valley) to be due to economic reasons that include "availability of lands," "opportunities to produce," and "opportunities to get rich." Bergmann (1966) has since verified the high degree of economic rationality and commercial orientation of the resettled highland peasants in the Santa Cruz area.

Bergmann's analysis leads us to consider determinants of rural settlement at the national level. Her conclusions are strongly in favor of planned settlement and the accompanying infrastructural investments. Since the Bolivian government has based its policies of colonization and regional investment on similar conclusions, and since migrants have responded dramatically to government policies (as perceived through the media), it behooves us to reiterate her analysis. Before 1954 (the year the Santa Cruz-Cochabamba highway was completed), some 11 percent of Bolivian commodity imports were staples (sugar and rice). The tin industry had stagnated owing to fluctuating world prices accompanied by low reinvestment rates and featherbedding. Finally, political vulnerability of the Santa Cruz area was at a maximum because of the city's isolation from the

Bolivian centers of political power and its ties with Argentina and Brazil, both of whom had extended rail spurs to Santa Cruz. The Bolivian government, after a study of alternative routes, constructed a 312-mile paved road from Cochabamba to Santa Cruz and simultaneously began to encourage colonization of the area (Fifer 1967). The results were that a little over ten years later, rice and sugar grown in the Santa Cruz region were meeting all domestic demands, increases in agricultural and petroleum production had compensated for stagnation in the tin industry, and political problems were largely nullified owing to increased ties with La Paz coupled with lowland settlement by Bolivians. Despite early failures, in-migration had brought about a doubling of Santa Cruz's population and increased momentum for further colonization in the adjacent area.

These public benefits of in-migration to a resource frontier (e.g., import substitution, economic diversification, and the solution to some portion of urban unemployment problem) provide incentives for public investment in peripheral roads and colonization among Andean countries. The Colombian government's efforts to colonize the Eastern Llanos (especially through road development—see Tinnermeier 1964) resulted in almost 400,000 in-migrants between 1951 and 1964 (Adams 1969).

In Venezuela, post-World War II agricultural colonization projects such as Turén and Majaguas in Portuguesa state have illustrated the aforementioned benefits in action; Turén provides the heart of the sesame- and rice-producing industry in the country (Hill and Beltran 1952; Miller 1966), and Majaguas serves the social needs of land redistribution among poor peasants (Leahy and Crist 1969). More important, the Venezuelan government has invested vast sums through the Guayana Development Corporation (CVG) in its Guayana region and through its petroleum subsidiary (CVP) and other subsidiaries in its Maracaibo region (e.g., the Morón and El Tablazo petroleum plants). Migrants have responded strongly to these economic incentives, easing somewhat the population pressures in the Andes.

In summary, in Venezuela (as elsewhere in Latin America) the existence of new migration magnets at the resource peripheries is forcing us to reexamine the motives for interregional migration in response to regional opportunities. Just how young Venezuelan migrants have responded to urban core versus resource periphery is the subject of the next section.

The Role of Perception

The *perception of opportunities*, rather than the opportunities themselves, determines the decision to migrate (see Lee 1966). Figure 1 illustrates how

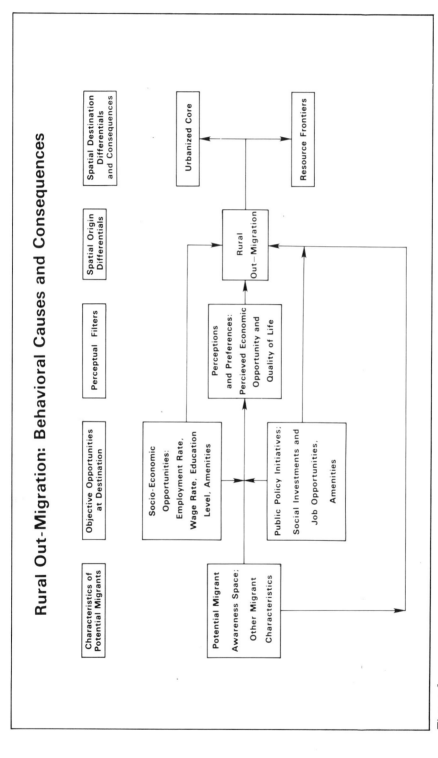

Rural Out-Migration: Behavioral Causes and Consequences

Characteristics of Potential Migrants

Objective Opportunities at Destination

Perceptual Filters

Spatial Origin Differentials

Spatial Destination Differentials and Consequences

Potential Migrant Awareness Space: Other Migrant Characteristics

Socio-Economic Opportunities: Employment Rate, Wage Rate, Education Level, Amenities

Public Policy Initiatives: Social Investments and Job Opportunities, Amenities

Perceptions and Preferences: Percieved Economic Opportunity and Quality of Life

Rural Out—Migration

Urbanized Core

Resource Frontiers

Figure 1

perceptual filters operate to shape the migration process. One type of filter is the myth map of potential destinations which potential migrants retain in their heads. The term *myth map* refers to an isoline map of the divergence between regional residential preferences and objective regional benefits. That such myth maps exist to a pronounced degree in Venezuela is probable, judging from the existence of urban congestion on the one hand and unexploited rural areas on the other.

One hundred ninety-one Venezuelan senior university students at five locations were interviewed in June 1974 and served as a sample of potential migrants (Figure 2). The locations represent the five major out-migration states (accounting for 43 percent of the total lifetime out-migrants in the counry). The students, from all parts of their respective states, were between sixteen and twenty-three years old (median age seventeen). They were each asked to rank thirty Venezuelan cities (Figure 3) on two criteria:

Where could you most easily find work?

Where could you find the most desirable physical and social environment (quality of life)?

These perceptual profiles were converted by the technique of principal components analysis (Gould and White 1974) to two group-agreement indices in which each city has a score, that is: (a) a 1 to 100 index of perceived economic opportunity (E), and (b) a 1 to 100 index of perceived quality of life (Q). These, then, are the *perceived opportunities.* The actual or *objective opportunities* for the thirty cities include five economic variables—three measures of unemployment rate (U_1, U_2, U_3), mean personal income per capita (Y), and standard deviation of mean family income (I); five quality-of-life variables—aggregate distance from out-migration zones (D), crime rate (C), tourist attractiveness (A), mean annual temperature (T), and education level (S); and the variable population size (P), which is considered both an economic and a quality-of-life variable. These eleven variables were obtained from Venezuelan government publications.

The myth maps were made operational by isoline mapping of the perceptual error terms, *e* and *d,* in

$$E = f(U_1, U_2, U_3, Y, I, P; e)$$
$$Q = g(D, C, A, T, S, P; d)$$

Thus, the myth maps represent the variation in *perceived* opportunities (E and Q) which cannot be explained by the *objective* opportunities that exist in the cities. It is hypothesized that the potential migrants will perceive both sets of opportunities as lower than they actually are in the Llanos

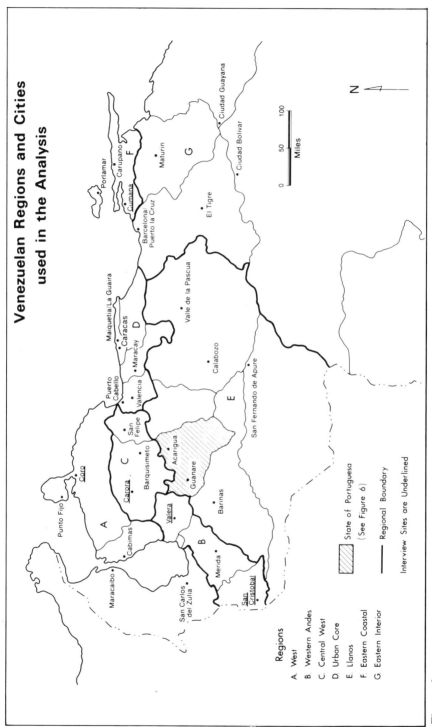

Venezuelan Regions and Cities used in the Analysis

Regions

A. West
B. Western Andes
C. Central West
D. Urban Core
E. Llanos
F. Eastern Coastal
G. Eastern Interior

State of Portuguesa (See Figure 6)

—— Regional Boundary

Interview Sites are Underlined

Figure 2

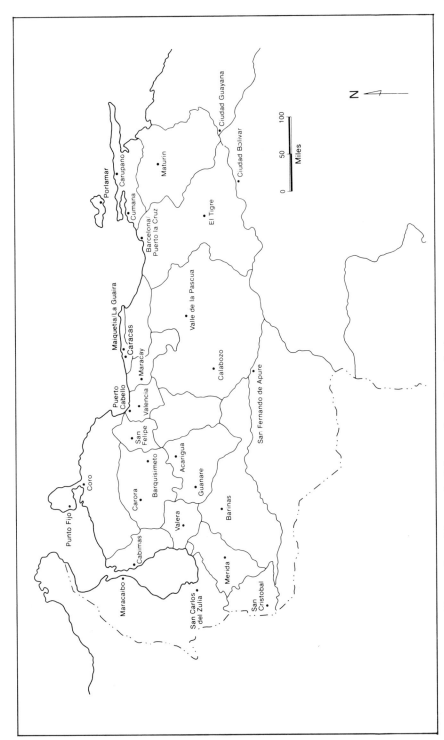

Figure 3. The thirty Venezuelan cities ranked by students in analysis.

and as higher than in the urban core and in the recreational western Andes and eastern coastal regions (Figure 2). Assuming we can map urban space, as distinct from total space, which would include rural areas, our resultant myth maps for economic opportunity (Figure 4) and quality of life (Figure 5) are similar to each other, as we would expect from the students' desire to minimize cognitive dissonance. There is a general perceptual gradient from southeast (low) to northwest (high). Such cities as Ciudad Bolívar, Barquísimeto, and Maracaibo stand out as pronounced peaks of overestimation of both types of opportunity. The visual impression is generally verified by a table of mean residual values (Table 1).

The maps possess considerable plausibility relative to what has been found for U. S. student mental maps (unusually high preferences for recreational areas, low ones for the Plains and specific Eastern urban centers). The Venezuelan students' unusually high preferences for peripheral industrial centers and for the urban core, however, are different from the U. S. case.

Do these myth maps hold any more than curiosity for us? The contents of such maps may exert an important influence on urban in-migration, regardless of what the actual opportunities in the urban centers may be. There is a certain proportion of urban in-migration which can never be explained by objective characteristics alone. It is suspected that myth-map biases may be responsible for this proportion. This suspicion may be tested by a model in which recent urban in-migration of fifteen- to twenty-four-year-olds is regressed, controlling for the objective opportunities present in the urban areas, against the myth-map surfaces for the cities. The results show that approximately 23 percent can be explained by the perceived economic opportunity index and 33 percent by the perceived quality-of-life index (Figure 6). This is a significant explanation of a phenomenon which cannot be understood from migration models that employ only objective characteristics (e.g., Levy and Wadycki 1972a, 1972b; Sahota 1968).

The Role of Mass Media, Kinship Ties, and Residential Experience

The myth maps of Venezuelan students (Figures 4 and 5) provide some insight into the important role played by the mass media in projecting favorable or unfavorable regional images. Consider the role of newspapers, which have in recent years popularized the regional development efforts of the public sector in Venezuela. Scattered issues of newspapers such as *El Nacional* (Caracas), *El Universal* (Caracas) and *Impulso* (Barquisimeto) were surveyed (1972–1974), and four themes emerge:

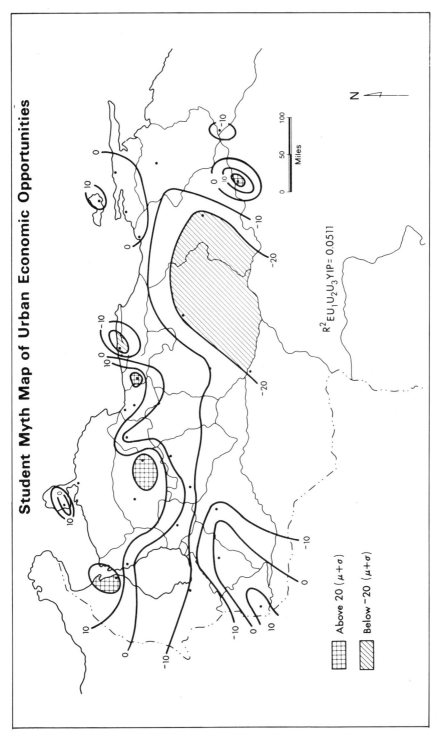

Student Myth Map of Urban Economic Opportunities

$R^2 EU_1 U_2 U_3 YIP = 0.0511$

Above 20 $(\mu + \sigma)$

Below -20 $(\mu + \sigma)$

0   50   100
Miles

N

Figure 4

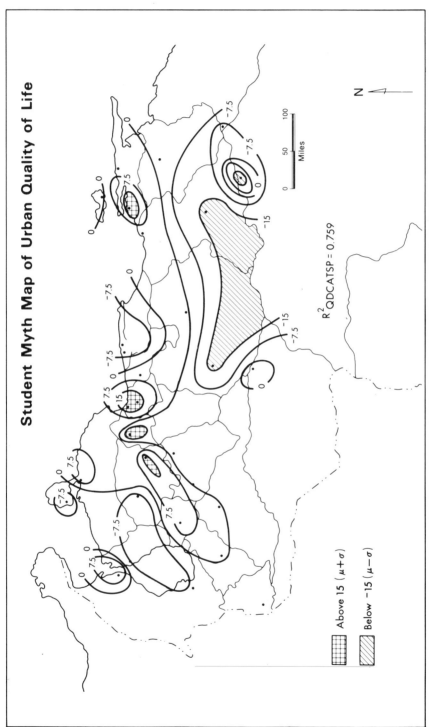

Figure 5

Table 1. Mean Residuals for Regional Groupings of Cities[a]

| Hypothesized Direction of Relationship | Region | No. of Cities | Misperception[b] of | |
			Economic Opportunity	Quality of Life
−	Llanos	6	−9.12	−3.01
+	Urban core	5	−0.57	+3.58
+	W. Andes/E. Coast	7	+2.88	+2.35

[a] Mean for all 30 cities; = 0.0
[b] A minus sign indicates the situation where perceived opportunities are less than those predicted from the objective variables; a plus sign indicates the situation where perceived opportunities are greater than predicted from the objective variables.
Source: Jones (1976).

1. Industrial developments in the eastern and western frontiers (iron ore and petroleum, respectively) have transformed resource peripheries into the new El Dorados.
2. The federal government has given financial encouragement for industries to decentralize from the urban core to the periphery; it also has decreed(1974) that new industries be established outside the metropolitan area of Caracas.
3. The scenic nature of the western Andes and the eastern coastal region have been actively promoted, with the intention of drawing Venezuelan and foreign tourists.
4. Life in the agricultural periphery (especially the Western and Central Llanos) has been viewed with an equal mix of paternalism and pity. This is partly evident from programs designed to eradicate rural slum dwellings or to help out the poor peasant families who are at the mercy of the elements. It is also evident in news accounts of agricultural setbacks in the Llanos followed by lack of government concern and in peasant jokes and cartoons.

Given these newspaper accounts, it is easier to understand why students overestimate opportunities in the Maracaibo region and in Ciudad Bolivar, overestimate opportunities in the east and the Andes, and underestimate opportunities in the Llanos.

In an attempt to determine quantitatively the impact of personal attributes (including sex, residential experience, kinship ties, career and income aspirations, and media contact) on personal preferences for the primate city (Caracas) as opposed to a rural growth center (Acarigua),

Table 2.   One-Way Analyses of Variance for the Relationship between Urban

Number
of Respondents

Hypothesis	Personal Attributes	with Attribute	without Attribute
H₁	Male	95	85
H₂	Rural birthplace	33	147
H₂	Rural residence of parents	22	158
H₂	Rural previous residence	43	137
H₂	Rural res. of siblings	94	86
H₂	Urban-core birthplace	12	168
H₂	Urban-core parents' res.	3	177
H₂	Urban-core previous res.	22	158
H₂	Urban-core siblings res.	43	137
H₃	Lowest income aspiration	106	74
H₃	Agricultural career aspir.	17	163
H₃	Highest income aspiration	29	151
H₃	Professional career aspir.	38	142
H₄	Urban-core newspaper	130	50
H₄	Urban-core radio	25	155

ᵃF—statistics for which the means support the hypotheses are italicized; relative to the means, a high value indicates a low mean preference for the city, and vice versa.

one study advanced a series of hypotheses: (a) females would prefer Caracas more than males (the converse of Acarigua) (H_1); (b) respondents with urban backgrounds and kinship ties would prefer Caracas more than other respondents (the converse for Acarigua, relative to rural background and ties) (H_2); (c) respondents with high income aspirations or professional career aspirations would prefer Caracas more than other respondents (the converse for Acarigua, relative to the opposite aspirations) (H_3); (d) respondents whose first choice was an urban-core newspaper or urban-core radio station, as opposed to a local newspaper or station, would prefer Caracas more than other respondents (the converse for Acarigua) (H_4) (Jones 1975). The results tend to verify the strong role which is played by residential experience, kinship ties, career aspirations, and particularly by newspaper or radio contact with the capital city (Table 2). The causal direction of such relationships cannot, of course, be established clearly from such results.

Still another Venezuelan study (Jones and Zannaras 1972) focused, on a smaller scale, on the residential preferences of fifty-three migrants to three towns in Portuguesa in the Western Llanos (Figures 2 and 7). The basic purpose was to find out whether a beneficial migration stream was

Preference and Personal Attributes of Potential Migrants[a]

Preferences for Acarigua			Preferences for Caracas		
Mean: with Attribute	Mean: without Attribute	F	Mean: with Attribute	Mean: without Attribute	F
16.64	16.54	.01	9.78	8.07	*1.56*
13.55	17.28	*5.88*[b]			
13.77	16.99	*3.08*[c]			
14.77	17.17	*2.91*[c]			
17.17	15.77	1.00			
			4.58	9.29	*2.97*[c]
			3.00	9.07	*1.29*
			6.55	9.31	*1.76*[c]
			6.79	9.66	*3.23*
16.28	17.04	*.38*			
13.65	16.90	*2.51*			
			9.14	8.40	.01
			6.89	9.53	*2.48*
16.85	15.92	*.48*	7.62	12.48	*10.64*[b]
14.96	16.86	1.19	5.36	9.55	*4.58*[b]

[b] Significant at 0.05 ($F_{1,178} = 3.90$).
[c] Significant at 0.10 ($F_{1,178} = 2.74$).
Source: Jones (1975).

threatened by the existence of latent out-migration potential. Preferences for larger, farther-away places (made operational via an index for size preference and for proximity preference, calculated for each respondent) were found to exist to a high degree among migrants to Turén, one of the most successful agricultural colonies in Latin America, while residents of the somewhat backward nearby rural town of Piritú possessed much more constricted preference spaces. It was hypothesized that socioeconomic status and urban residential experience would be positively related to preference for larger, farther-away places. The results indicate that a respondent's history of migration to a larger place and his identification of his original migration motive as "economic factors at the destination" were significantly important influences on preferences (Table 3).

This research suggests that colonization authorities may face a dilemma. Should they encourage in-migration to the Western Llanos of individuals who are accustomed to a rural way of life (but who have low socioeconomic status), or should they encourage in-migration of individuals of higher education and income levels who are apt to leave when conditions worsen at the destination? Either of these may be viable policy alternatives

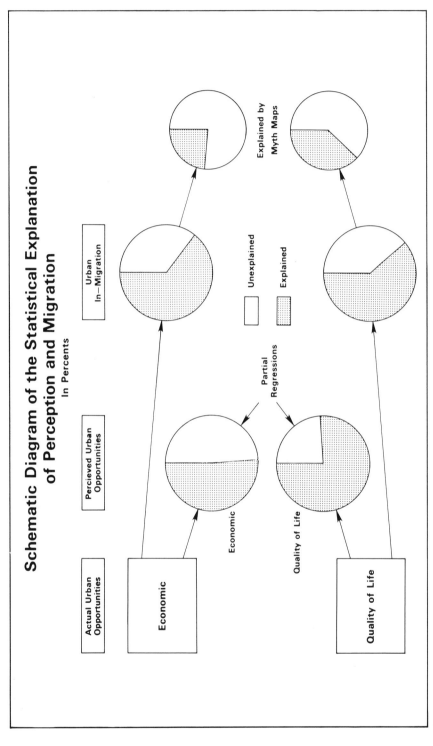

Figure 6

Internal Structure of the State of Portuguesa, Venezuela

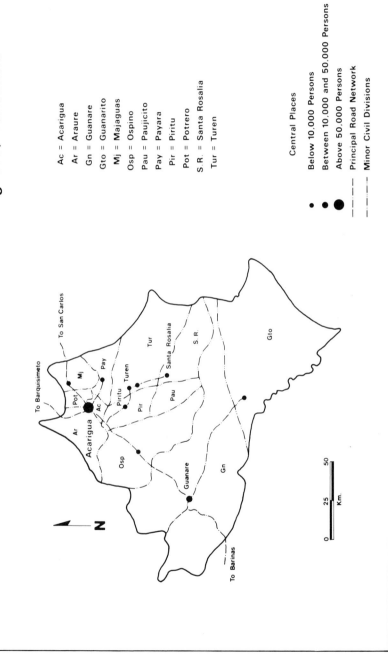

Ac = Acarigua
Ar = Araure
Gn = Guanare
Gto = Guanarito
Mj = Majaguas
Osp = Ospino
Pau = Paujicito
Pay = Payara
Pir = Piritu
Pot = Potrero
S.R. = Santa Rosalia
Tur = Turen

Central Places

Below 10,000 Persons
Between 10,000 and 50,000 Persons
Above 50,000 Persons
Principal Road Network
Minor Civil Divisions

Figure 7

Table 3. Standardized Partial Regression Coefficients: Analysis of Preferences for Larger and Closer Cities, Western Llanos[a]

| | Hypothesized Direction of Relationship | | Coefficients | |
Independent Variable	Size	Proximity	Size	Proximity
Age	−	+	−.003	+.153
Male sex [b]	−	+	−.024	−.148
Family size	−	+	+.070	−.279 [c]
Larger birthplace [b]	+	−	+.396 [c]	−.362 [c]
Larger prior residence [b]	+	−	+.181	−.193
Move for economic "pull" [b]	+	−	+.347 [c]	−.429 [c]
Distance of prior move	+	−	+.149	−.075
Education	+	−	+.016	−.150
Income	+	−	+.167	−.101
Nonagricultural occupation [b]	+	−	+.109	−.236
R² for all ten independent variables			.65	.80

[a] Standardized $bj = Bj = bj\frac{sj}{si}$, where sj, si = standard deviations of independent, dependent variables; bj = raw regression coefficient
[b] Dichotomous variable.
[c] Significantly different from zero at the 0.05 level ($F_{10,19}$).
Source: Jones and Zannaras (1972).

if on-the-site training or provision of urban amenities is forthcoming from the public sector.

Consequences of Rural Urban Migration: An On-Going Controversy

In the literature, there is no consensus on whether the consequences of rural migration into large urban areas are favorable or unfavorable for the individuals involved, the two regions involved, or for the country as a whole. Urban anthropologist William Mangin supports the contention that benefits to the individual and to society from migration to squatter settlements in large urban areas are strongly positive. Specifically, he cannot accept the "myths" of squatter settlements as foci for urban crime, family breakdown, illiteracy, radicalism, and parasitism. He argues that "the formation of squatter settlements is a popular response to rapid urbanization in countries that cannot or will not provide services for the increasing urban population" (Mangin 1967). Sociologists Gino Germani (1961) and Rafael Cardona (Cardona and Simmons 1973) see cities in general and marginal slum settlements in particular as mechanisms for modernization through effective participation in and integration into the national society.

As far as they go, these arguments appear to be theoretically valid and realistic. Some researchers, however, have been critical of the Mangin school of thought on three grounds: (a) particular case studies do not agree with Mangin's conclusions for Peru; (b) the individual opportunity costs of nonmigration to the resource periphery are ignored; and (c) the costs to society as a whole are not adequately assessed. For example, political scientist Talton Ray, writing on Venezuelan barrios, comes to several conclusions at odds with Mangin's. Migrants to Venezuelan cities tend to arrive unemployed and remain so for long periods. Underemployment reaches 70 percent in slums of Gabimas in the western oil field when oil production slows down, and it is commonly 15 to 20 percent in Caracas, Valencia, and Ciudad Guayana. Barrio businesses are marginal, contributing little to the urban or national economy. Finally, the impact of barrio residents on the growth of commercial and industrial activity in cities is weak (Ray 1969). In addition, several studies focus on the negative impacts on zones of emigration of the exodus of ambitious, talented people (Preston 1969, 1974; Adams 1969; Bradfield 1973); if one accepts emigration from rural areas as irreversible, then he can hardly forget about costs to those remaining behind when evaluating benefits to those who move to squatter settlements.

The second argument at odds with the Mangin school of thought has to do with the costs and benefits to society of migration to urban areas instead of to resource frontiers. In the cases where resource zones are yet to be tapped, where foodstuffs are imported, and where the government is placing considerable investments in the peripheral areas (agricultural research and extension, credit, land clearing, etc.), the opportunity costs of noncolonization of the resource periphery may be positive and substantial, for the individual and for the whole society (Crist and Nissly 1973; Adams 1968, 1969; Bergmann 1966). Conversely, the emigration of former in-migrants to the resource periphery may have a strongly negative impact for both the individual and for the society at large.

It is possible, on the other hand, that the net benefits of movement to a metropolis will be positive to the in-migrant while negative to the society (and that the converse will hold for movement into a resource frontier). This situation brings us to the third counterargument to the Mangin school of thought, as analyzed by Bruce Herrick:

If the world were characterized by equality of individual and social products, fewer analytical problems with respect to the economic effects of urbanization would arise. The urban migrants would earn their marginal product in the cities, their presence neither benefiting nor injuring those already there. However, . . . the migrant imposes costs on others which he need not pay. The well-known urban characteristics associated with population density such as physical crowding, transportation congestion, and air pollution all might be partly attributed to unchecked inflows of urban workers and their families, responding to private incentives. (Herrick 1971, pp. 76–77)

In another study, Benjamin Higgins, analyzing what he terms "urbanization without industrialization," outlines a series of costly negative externalities for in-migration to large cities: (a) intensified regional dualism and its attendant problems for regional specialization and economic interactions; (b) aggravation of underemployment in the monetized urban sector; and (c) denudation of leadership from rural zones (Higgins 1967; also see Friedman 1966, chapter 10).

Evidence strongly suggests that rural growth centers are developing in the resource peripheries of the North Andean countries, concomitantly with continued growth of large urban areas (Preston 1969), and it appears that this trend will continue. As it does, the relative costs and benefits of peripheral investments will become better known as projects now underway reach fruition. Judged initially, schemes to develop Brasília, Ciudad Guayana, Santa Cruz, and other new towns were not notably successful, but time has revealed unforeseen benefits. Conversely, time has revealed unforeseen costs to continued urban in-migration. Nevertheless, the conflict between the two theories—the Mangin /Germani notion of the city as an integrating mechanism, and the Herrick/Higgins notion of the city as a social burden—has yet to be resolved.

Implications of the Research

One conclusion from the study is that much of the academic and planning community has been overly concerned with what is happening in the cities of Latin America and too little concerned with what goes on in intermediate-sized and smaller cities in the resource peripheries. Reading anthropological and sociological literature, one cannot avoid the argument that migration to large cities is rational because individual migrants benefit from it; and if individuals benefit, so must society. Macroscale studies which calculate either the externalities or the opportunity costs to society as a whole or to urban in-migration are seldom found or attempted even in a qualitative sense; yet it appears that these externalities may be negative for movement into primate cities and positive for movement into resource frontiers. One who follows the newspapers in Latin America cannot fail to be impressed with their highly pragmatic, development-oriented journalism, and most of it is directed to new ventures in the resource peripheries, for example, the dedication of a new dam or road, the contracting of new international markets for a petrochemical plant, a dramatic move by the government to decentralize production of manufactured goods, an investment in agricultural research designed to revolutionize yields, etc. These accounts have caught the popular fancy and pride in Venezuela as elsewhere and have led to a steadily increasing migration stream to the "innovative periphery."

Another conclusion from this study is that existing research on the motives of migration has focused too exclusively on the relationship between aggregate migration streams and objective characteristics of migrants and places. More research on the intervening roles played by media contact, kinship ties, and residential experiences as they influence urban preferences of potential migrants appears justified. As Julian Wolpert has so eloquently pointed out,

> Population migration. . .differs in certain essential characteristics from other channels of interaction, mainly in terms of the commodity which is being transported. With migration, the agent which is being transported is itself active and generates its own flow. The origin and destination points take on significance only in the framework in which they are perceived by the active agents. (Wolpert 1965, p. 161)

From the point of view of policy implications, it does not appear extreme to suggest that an official attempt to influence attitudes and to change misconceptions held by potential migrants might prove more efficient and cheaper than the present policy of extensive infrastructural investments in rural and urban areas. A definitive answer to whether this is the case will depend on the answers to several questions:

1. What are the comparative long-run benefits and costs to society of peripheral versus core-regional migration?
2. What are the minimum amenity and wage thresholds for migra- tion to and permanence in rural resource zones?
3. Are media messages able to influence significantly decisions to migrate (or not to migrate), controlling for such elements as kinship, ties, residential experiences, aspirations, and status?
4. Are short-run favoritisms for certain regions or segments of population and want-deferment for others viable (or possible)

political strategies under the assumption of long-run benefits to society as a whole?

References

Adams, Dale W. 1968. "Leadership, Education, and Agricultural Development Programs in Colombia." *Inter-American Economic Affairs*, 22:87-96.

Adams, Dale W. 1969. "Rural Migration and Agricultural Development in Colombia." *Economic Development and Cultural Change*, 17:527-39.

Bergmann, Barbara R. 1966. "The Cochabamba-Santa Cruz Highway in Bolivia." In *The Impact of Highway Investment on Development*, George Wilson, et al., (eds.), Washington, D.C.: Brookings, pp. 17-54.

Bradfield, Stillman. 1973. "Selectivity in Rural-Urban Migration: The Case of Huaylas, Peru." In *Urban Anthropology: Cross-Cultural Studies of Urbanization,* Aidan Southall and E. M. Bruner (eds.), New York: Oxford University Press, 1973, pp. 351-372.

Cardona, Ramiro C. and Alan B. Simmons. 1973. "Apuntes Sobre la Llamada 'Crisis' en las Grandes Ciudades." *Monografías de la Corporación Centro Regional de Población*, 1 (December).

Carvajal, Manuel J. and David T. Geithman. 1974. "An Economic Analysis of Migration in Costa Rica." *Economic Development and Cultural Change*, 23:1959. 105-122.

Cisneros, Cesar C. 1959. "Indian Migration from the Andean Zone of Ecuador to the Lowlands." *America Indigena*, 19:225-31.

Crist, Raymond E. and Charles M. Nissly. 1973. *East from the Andes.* University of Florida Social Sciences Monograph No. 50. Gainesville: University of Florida Press.

Fifer, J. Valerie. 1967. "Bolivia's Pioneer Fringe." *The Geographical Review*, 57: 1-23.

Flinn, William L. 1966. "Rural to Urban Migration: A Colombian Case." *Land Tenure Center Research paper No. 19*, Madison: University of Wisconsin Press.

Flinn, William L. and David G. Cartano. 1970. "A Comparison of the Migration Process to An Urban Barrio and to a Rural Community: Two Case Studies." *Inter-American Economic Affairs*, 24:37-48

Friedmann, John. 1966. *Regional Development Policy: A Case Study of Venezuela.* Cambridge, Mass.: MIT Press.

Gakenheimer, Ralph A. 1967. "The Peruvian City of the Sixteenth Century." In *The Urban Explosion in Latin America*, Glenn H. Beyer (ed.), Ithaca, N.Y.: Cornell University Press, pp. 33-56.

Germani, Gino. 1961. "Inquiry into the Social Effects of Urbanization in a Working Class Sector of Greater Buenos Aires." In *Urbanization in Latin America*, Philip Hauser (ed.), Ithaca N.Y: Cornell University Press, pp. 206-33.

Gould, Peter and Rodney White. 1974. *Mental Maps*, Baltimore: Penguin Press.

Herrick, Bruce. 1971. "Urbanization and Urban Migration in Latin America: An

Economist's View." In *Latin American Urban Research*, Vol. I, F. Rabi-
novitz and F. Trueblood (eds.), Beverly Hills, Calif.: Sage Publications,
pp. 71–81.

Higgins, Benjamin. 1967. "Urbanization, Industrialization, and Economic Development." In *The Urban Explosion in Latin America*, Glenn Beyer (ed.),
Ithaca, N.Y.: Cornell University Press, pp. 117–55.

Hill, George W. and Gregorio Beltran. 1952. "Land Settlement in Venezuela with
Special Reference to the Turen Project," *Rural Sociology*, 17:229–36.

Jones, Richard C. 1975. "Latent Migration Potential Between a Depressed Region and Alternative Destinations: A Venezuelan Case Study," *Proceedings, AAG*, 7:104–09.

Jones, Richard C. and Georgia Zannaras. 1972. "In-Migration and Residential
Preferences in the Western Llanos of Venezuela." Paper read at the annual
meeting of the East Lakes Association of American Geographers (October), Indiana University, Indiana, Pennsylvania.

Leahy, Edward P. and Raymond E. Crist. 1969. "Agricultural Reform in the
Humid Tropics: The Example of Las Majaguas," *The Professional Geographer*, 21:8–10.

Lee, Everett S. 1966. "A Theory of Migration," *Demography*, 3:47–57.

Levy, Mildred B. and Walter J. Wadycki. 1972. "A Comparison of Young and
Middle-Aged Migration in Venezuela," *Annals of Regional Science*, 6:73–
85.

Levy, Mildred B. and Walter J. Wadycki. 1972. "Lifetime Versus One-Year
Migration in Venezuela," *Journal of Regional Science*, 12:407–15.

Mangin, William. 1967. "Latin American Squatter Settlements: A Problem and a
Solution," *Latin American Research Review*, 2:65–98.

Miller, E. Willard. 1968. "Population and Agricultural Development in the
Western Llanos of Venezuela," *Revista Geografica*, 69:7–23.

Preston, D[avid] A. 1969. "Rural Emigration in Andean America," *Human
Organization*, 28:279–86.

Preston, (David) A. 1974. "Emigration and Changes: Experience in Southern
Ecuador." Unpublished manuscript, Department of Geography, University of Leeds.

Ray, Talton F. 1969. *The Politics of the Barrios of Venezuela*. Berkeley: University of California Press.

Reina, Ruben E. 1964. "The Urban World View of a Tropical Forest Community
in the Absence of a City: Peten, Guatemala," *Human Organization*,
23:265–77.

Sahota, G. S. 1968. "An Economic Analysis of Internal Migration in Brazil,"
Journal of Political Economy, 76:218–45.

Sariola, Sakari. 1960. "A Colonization Experiment in Bolivia," *Rural Sociology*,
25:76–90.

Schultz, T. P. 1971. "Rural–Urban Migration in Colombia," *Review of Economics
and Statistics*, 53:157–63.

Tinnermeier, Ronald L. 1964. "New Land Settlement in the Eastern Lowlands of
Colombia." Land Tenure Center Research Paper No. 13. Madison: University of Wisconsin.

Wilkening, Eugene A. 1968. "Comparison of Migrants in Two Rural and an Urban Area of Central Brazil." Land Tenure Center Research Paper No. 35. Madison: University of Wisconsin.

Wolpert, Julian. 1965. "Behaviorial Aspects of the Decision to Migrate," *Papers and Proceedings* (Regional Science Association), 15:159–69.

Robert N. Thomas
and James L. Mulvihill

Temporal Attributes of
Stage Migration in Guatemala

The process of human migration from rural or urban areas has been described in numerous ways, including the stepwise thesis. Discussion of the process can be traced to the late 1800s, when migrations were observed to proceed by stages, each migrant filling a place left by another.[1] As stated then, "stepwise" and "stage" migrations were distinct processes. Stepwise migration assumed that an individual moves from a rural area to a primate city through a central-place hierarchy (Figure 1). Leaving the rural setting for a nearly rural village, the individual would move up in the hierarchy to a larger urban center and eventually arrive in the primate city. Stage migration, on the other hand, emphasized replacement, the individual moving from a secondary center to a primate city and being replaced in the secondary center by someone from a smaller city, and so on down the hierarchy (Figure 2).

The concepts of stepwise and stage migration assume a flow of information through a hierarchy of central places.[2] Because the information field of a lower-order village is more restricted than that of a higher-order center, such a village is less likely to experience significant out-migration. Its inhabitants are less aware of the attractivenes of major urban centers as their awareness is limited to the local center.

Of the various conceptual frameworks describing migration to intermediate centers, the most prominent is that of intervening opportunities. Stouffer proposes that the number of persons going a given distance is directly proportional to the number of opportunities at that distance and inversely proportional to the number of intervening opportunities.[3] In this context, the smaller secondary centers become intervening opportunities between the rural village and the larger urban centers. The relative attraction of the potential receiving centers is not only a function of the absolute number of opportunities existing there, but also a function of the potential migrant's awareness of them.

An African example outlines the behavioral view of the same process. It indicates that although job opportunities and the attraction of "bright

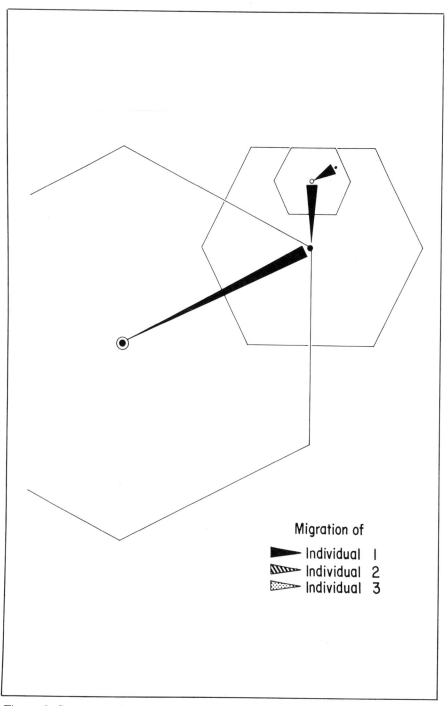

Migration of
Individual 1
Individual 2
Individual 3

Figure 1. Stepwise migration; individual moves from a rural area to a primate city.

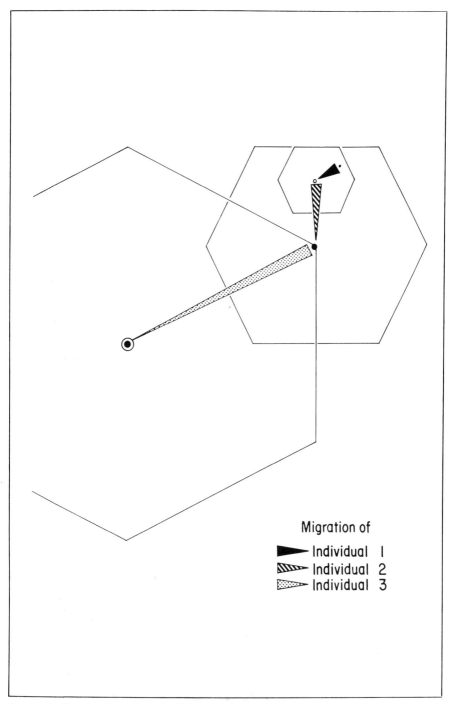

Figure 2. Stage migration; individual moves from secondary center to a primate city.

lights" are much fewer in small towns than in large cities, the smaller towns are more accessible culturally and socially as well as more practical in terms of time, cost, and energy.[4] Similarly, investigations of the migration process in Latin America have supported this contention of stage migration, or replacement. A Guatemalan study states that the majority of migrants arriving in Guatemala City come from one of the country's secondary urban centers. They in turn are replaced by migrants from other nearby rural areas and smaller towns.[5]

Distance and Stage Migration

Few studies testing the stage-migration thesis in Latin America have considered the effect of distance on the process of migration between rural and urban areas. Will stage migration apply to a migrant living fifty miles from a primate city as well as to one two hundred miles away? Will the rural component of the stage-migration system increase in importance as distance from the primate city increases? Although their research does not focus on the distance variable per se, Riddell and Harvey indicate that stage migration is apparent in areas distant from the major city.[6] They observe that African migrants who live in rural areas close to Freetown, Sierra Leone, do not move to closer medium-sized cities, but migrate directly to the primate city. In Guatemala, the same type of migration is indicated in a study by Thomas and Catau.[7] They found that the rural migrant living near a primate city skips the local secondary center and moves directly to the primate city, while a rural migrant living a considerable distance from the primate city is more likely to move to the local secondary center (Figure 3). The secondary center located close to a primate city is thus viewed as less of an intervening opportunity than is a more distant secondary center. It is assumed that the potential migrant living near the primate city is more familiar with the major urban center than is the potential migrant living at a greater distance. The individual living nearby probably visits the primate city more frequently and is more likely to have friends and relatives there who can assist in the assimilation process.

Although their research revealed this positive association between distance and the incidence of stage migration, the authors indicate that another vital concern could affect the role of the secondary urban centers in the stage-migration process. What influence, if any, does the element of time have upon the process? Does the potential migrant's information field expand with the tremendous growth in communications technology, as well as the increased capacity to utilize available information effec-

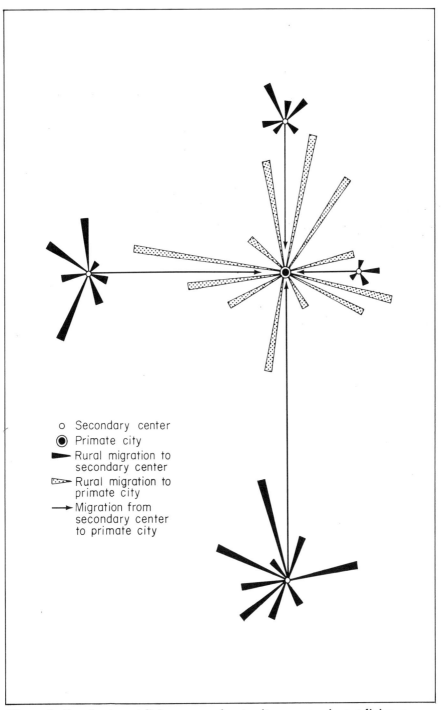

Figure 3. Rural migrant living near primate city versus migrant living a considerable distance from city.

tively? Is the potential migrant better able to receive and evaluate opportunities beyond his local secondary urban center? Can it be assumed that technological progress makes obsolete the theory of stage migration?

Problem and Hypothesis

Recent advances in techniques of communication and society's increasing ability to utilize them have extended the potential migrant's awareness of available opportunities. As information becomes more widely disseminated, the lure of secondary urban centers gives way to that of primate cities. In particular, the young, better-educated, and more highly skilled populations of secondary centers have abandoned their birthplaces and joined others of similar background in the rush to the primate city—hence the well-known "brain drain" and socioeconomic changes in many secondary centers in Central America. In general, the appeal of secondary centers as intervening opportunities probably diminishes, especially to the more ambitious potential migrant living in the countryside.

A time-space model, then, suggests the vital role of time in attempts to explain the process of stage migration. In the Guatemalan study, it was intuitively expected that the role of the secondary center as an intervening opportunity would change vis-à-vis both space and time. Figure 4 shows that in time period one (1), some rural migrants living near the primate center have already bypassed their local secondary center for the primate city, while rural migrants in areas B, C, and D still view their local secondary center as a viable intervening opportunity and move there.

In the intermediate time period, time period two (2), the secondary urban centers in areas both A and B are bypassed by rural migrants who move directly to the primate city. By now, communication systems of the primate city have reached out to these more distant rural areas, beckoning populations to join the migrant streams to the primate city. This call to the potential rural migrant is more likely to be heard and heeded if the local secondary center lacks social and economic services.

Finally, in time period 3 (3), the present, rural migrants are moving directly to the primate city from all parts of the country. Even in the most distant areas, the local secondary centers no longer act as important intervening opportunities for nearby rural migrants. The song of the primate city is instilled in the faintest of rural hearts, encouraging their flight to join the rural brothers and sisters in the big city.

This hypothesis is tested in the following form: Today, migrants arriving in a primate city are more likely than in the past to have come directly from a rural environment.

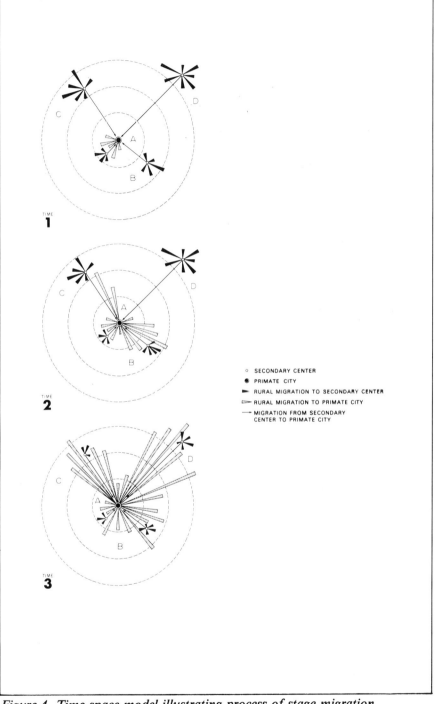

Figure 4. Time-space model illustrating process of stage migration.

Sampling Procedure

Migrant information from the Guatemalan national census provides insufficient data to answer the specific question raised in the study. To investigate the process of internal migration to Guatemala City and to make comparisons between rural and urban migrants, a questionnaire was administered to 2,500 family heads, representing 2.5 percent of family heads in Guatemala City.[8] The selection of the address of each family head was determined by stratified random sampling; i.e., the sample was stratified by zones and random within each zone. Thus, since zone 2 contains 4.23 percent of the families in the capital, 4.23 percent of the 2,500 samples, or 106 interviews, were conducted in zone 2, and so forth. The most accurate list of addresses of family units in Guatemala City was provided by official Guatemalan census questionnaires. To ensure open selection of any given family address, a list of random numbers was employed.[9]

Data Analysis

Of the total 2,500 family units visited, approximately 1,200 migrant family heads were interviewed for their migration history. For this study, it was specifically necessary to know the migrants' last place of residence prior to their moves to Guatemala City. These data were divided into three categories according to the year of migration to the capital: (a) those who came prior to 1946, (b) those who arrived between 1946 and 1955, and (c) those who moved to the city from 1956 to 1965. For each of Guatemala's twenty-one departments, exclusive of the Department of Guatemala, in which Guatemala City is located, the number of migrants originating in the department capital (the *cabecera*) was recorded as a percentage of the number of migrants from that department as a whole. The first variable—the dependent variable—indicates the relative magnitude of migration to Guatemala City for each department capital in relation to the total number of migrants from that department. The second variable is that of highway distance between Guatemala City and each *cabecera*. It is postulated that as highway distance increases, the incidence of stage migration increases.

Three regression analyses were obtained by using the percentage of migrants originating in each *cabecera* as the dependent variable and the common logarithm of highway distance as the independent variable (Table 1). The results reveal several significant features about the migration system and its change through time. First, the positive regression coefficients indicate that in all three periods studied, the importance of the

Table 1. Results of Regression Analysis

	Regression Coefficients	Correlation Coefficients	R^2
(1) Prior to 1946	.4985	.648	.420
(2) 1946 to 1955	.4550	.554	.306
(3) 1956 to 1965	.3148	.414	.171

cabeceras' contributions to individual migration streams increased with distance from Guatemala City; as is indicated in Figure 3, the attraction of the secondary center as an intervening opportunity increased in direct proportion to the distance from the primate city. Second, although distance continued to influence the strength of the cabeceras' contributions to a departmental migration stream, their role had a gradually diminishing effect; for each time period, the value of the regression coefficients declined. Lastly, Table 1 points out that the coefficients of determination (R^2) are lower for time period three (3), the present, than for time period one (1). This indicates a similar decline in the significance of distance, implying that other variables, not included in this study, have become increasingly important.

These findings verify the hypothesis that today a greater proportion of migrants arriving in a primate city have come directly from a rural area than in the past. This could indicate the demisc of stage migration to primate cities.

Suggestions for Further Study

Although the simplicity of the above analysis is attractive, certain shortcomings must be acknowledged. Foremost is the question of other influential variables. Although the availability and utilization of information are difficult to measure, appropriate surrogates are to be found in literacy rates, average income data, and the proportion of a department's population living in its cabecera. Relative migrant contribution of the department capital and the department in general have been compared; perhaps the relative disparities in these variables should be considered. One might hypothesize that the greater the disparity in levels of social and economic development between cabecera and department, the greater the percentage of migrants to leave the cabecera. It is assumed that the more developed a department, the fewer the disparities between cabecera and noncabecera and the more uniform the availability of information. Other variables for possible use in future model-building could include distance to a major (paved) highway, average income, proportion of Indians to total population, and the proximity of a department capital to a strong intervening opportunity. As stated above, the importance of these variables may be not their absolute magnitude, but rather the disparity of their incidence in *cabeceras* and non*cabeceras*.

Although it would be difficult to undertake a subdepartment (*municipio*) scale of analysis, the results might give a more exact indication of other variables to be included. The department level of aggregation used here limits the precision of interpretation.

Implications of the Study

These findings reveal an aspect of the migration process that should interest policy-making officials. It is apparent that the typical migrant to a primate city today is more likely to have moved directly from the countryside than were past migrants, who typically came from one of the secondary urban centers. Several policy conclusions stem from this change.

Today's newly arrived migrants are less equipped for rapid assimilation into the social, economic, and political life of the primate city than were their predecessors since they have come directly from the countryside, and the lack of previous urban experience makes adjustment to urban living difficult. In the past, the newly arrived migrants settled initially in "gateway barrios," communities of others like themselves clustered in the foreign urban environment. This formation of rural villages within the city has become even more pronounced today and should be of particular interest to social agencies. The new migrants need social and economic services such as job training, job placement, health programs, family care programs, family planning services, and pre- and postnatal clinics.

Thought could also be given to encouraging potential migrants to remain in their home area. This might be accomplished by a review of land-tenure systems and farm consolidations of fragmented land parcels, and a reexamination of migration from one rural area to another as a satisfactory answer to a migrant's desire for an improved life. Such colonization programs, dependent on government action, need to receive greater emphasis by Central American governments.

National governments could also encourage local agricultural communities to form cooperatives and to pool their efforts by specializing in the production, processing, and marketing of specific agricultural products. Such combined and specialized efforts usually result in superior products for a ready market, national or international, and improve the economic productivity of the cooperative members.

A greater share of the country's resources could also be assigned to secondary urban centers. By this means, these smaller urban places could be vitalized socially and economically and so enabled to resume the role of viable intervening opportunities for potential migrants in the rural areas. Local planning groups in the secondary centers could be established to assess present urban resources and to formulate a local priority system for developmental projects. Then, in order that their developmental goals be accomplished, national governments must be made aware of the need to allocate a greater share of the country's financial resources to these secondary urban centers.

These are but a few of the possibilities of investigation for development planners in Guatemala and other countries of Central America. Once the impact of the stage-migration process and its imminent demise are understood, national and regional planners should initiate policies to assist in solving migration-associated problems at all levels of the urban hierarchy.

Notes

1. E. G. Ravenstein, "The Laws of Migration," *Journal of the Royal Statistical Society* 48, pt. 2 (1885): 167–227.
2. Gunnar Olsson, *Distance and Human Interaction: A Review and Bibliography* (Philadelphia: Regional Science Research Institute, 1965), pp. 30–32.
3. Samuel A. Stouffer, "Intervening Opportunities: A Theory Relating Mobility and Distance," *American Sociological Review* 5 (1940): 846.
4. J. Barry Riddell and Milton E. Harvey, "The Urban System in the Migration Process: An Evaluation of Step-Wise Migration in Sierra Leone," *Economic Geography* 48 (1972): 272.
5. Robert N. Thomas, "The Migration System of Guatemala City: Spatial Aspects," *The Professional Geographer* 24 (1972): 109–10.
6. Riddell and Harvey, "Urban System," p. 279, footnote 4.
7. Robert N. Thomas and John C. Catau, "Distance and the Incidence of Step-Wise Migration in Guatemala," *Proceedings of the Association of American Geographers*, 6 (1974): 113–16.
8. Robert N. Thomas, "Survey Research Design: A Case of Rural-Urban Mobility," in *Geographic Research on Latin America: Benchmark 1970*, Barry Lentnek, Robert L. Carmin, and Tom L. Martinson, eds. (Muncie, Ind.: Ball State University Press, 1971), pp. 421–27.
9. Rand Corporation, *A Million Random Digits with 100,000 Normal Deviates* (Glencoe, Ill.: Free Press, 1955). Fieldwork was conducted in 1965–1966.

Stillman Bradfield
and Leila Bradfield

Migrant Receiving Centers in Developing Countries: The Case of Chimbote, Peru*

The simplest answer to the question "Why do people migrate to the cities?" is essentially the same as that given by the famous bank robber Willie Sutton, who, when asked by a reporter, "Why do you rob banks?" replied, "Because that's where the money is." People migrate from one place to another in the hope that they will be better off. They hope to be better off economically, but there are other motives, such as education for their children, the enjoyment of health, entertainment, and other urban facilities, and participation in the wider society.

In order to understand the desert coast of Peru some 415 kilometers north of Lima, we must look first at geographical factors in the area, and then to its history. As is true everywhere, resources mean different things at different times according to such factors as the current state of technology, transportation facilities, and markets. These in turn have to be viewed in comparison to alternative possibilities in the area.

A Brief Historical Sketch

Chimbote is located on a large bay in an offshoot of the Santa River Valley. Aerial photos reveal that the valley was more extensively cultivated in pre-Columbian times than at present. The Santa River is fed both by rains in the mountains and by the melting of glaciers in the Cordillera Blanca, and it flows year round. Because it virtually never rains on the coast of Peru, the combination of warm temperature, solar energy, and permanently available irrigation water makes the Santa Valley ideal for agriculture.

In pre-Columbian times, the Mochica-Chimu peoples inhabited this valley; they were one of the last cultures to be conquered by the Incas, shortly before the Incas were conquered by the Spanish. The fierce resistance put up by the inhabitants meant that the valley was virtually uninhabited at the time of the Spanish conquest. It was some time before agriculture really got started in the valley on any substantial scale, but over time haciendas were developed.

The place that is now Chimbote is on a well-protected, large bay with a deep harbor; it was first settled by six families of fishermen, who moved from Huanchaquito in the 1760s. Growth to 1870 was extremely slow, but in 1871, Chimbote was declared a major port, which permitted it to conduct foreign trade. Chimbote had long been considered an ideal place to locate a town, not only because of its natural advantages as a harbor, but because of the potential connections with the highly populated interior highlands. In 1871, Henry Meiggs, having convinced President Balta that railroads would do the same for the Peruvian interior as they had done to promote the development of the U.S. West, began a penetration railroad from Chimbote to Requay, at the upper end of the Santa Valley. After years, the railroad finally made it as far as Huallanca, and road transportation became available through the Callejon de Huaylas. As part payment for services on the railroad, Meiggs was given title to land at the port, and between 1871 and 1879 he and his brother laid out the town of Chimbote in the classic Spanish grid pattern, with wide streets, a few good buildings, and a central plaza. The initial purpose of the town was to export products from the interior, and houses were constructed for the officials of the railroad and the customs agency of the government at this time.

In the early 1880s, Chimbote was invaded by the Chileans, and considerable destruction ensued. As a result of damage done to the railroad, the port was closed and not reopened until the early 1920s. By 1924, water was still being hauled by train from the Santa River, but Chimbote had a few hotels, a small provisional chapel, several schools, electricity, a telegraph, and mail service. Some recreational facilities, such as a soccer field and tennis courts, allowed diversion for the population, which was estimated at about 2,000.

Struggles for control of the land in and around Chimbote began early. In 1927, an indigenous community was formed to hold land in common, assigning cultivation rights to individuals. This organization became the major land speculator until the 1970s, when it was finally abolished. But in the meantime, it competed with the Meiggs family, the city, and the Santa Corporation for control of the land and was able to speculate in land, even though the individuals concerned did not hold personally valid titles.

Agricultural land on the edge of Chimbote fluctuated in use and value according to how much water was available. This was a function not simply of the amount of water coming down the river, but of how much the haciendas in the Santa Valley permitted to flow in Chimbote. From 1925 to 1932, there was an adequate supply of water which allowed the expansion of agriculture on the edge of Chimbote, and as a result, considerable in-migration from haciendas in the Santa Valley took place to take advantage of the opportunity to appropriate this land at no cost. Throughout this period, migration was also encouraged by the change in several of the largest haciendas from sugar to cotton, which requires much less labor. Many of the displaced farm workers came to Chimbote at that time. Fights with the largest hacienda, Tamboreal, over water rights, led to Chimbote's losing one thousand hectares of agricultural land to the hacienda, retaining only eight hundred for its own use.

By 1934, the railroad began to pay off, as coal mined in the mountains was being shipped abroad, and the dock at Chimbote was working around the clock. This attracted more merchants and their shops to Chimbote; many of the Chinese who had been brought in to work on the railroad and their descendants quickly came to dominate commerce. A few Arabs and Germans came in the late 1920s and early 1930s, and they later became prominent business people in Chimbote.

Until 1940, all shipping in and out of Chimbote was by sea, but in that year the Pan-American Highway was completed, connecting Lima with Chimbote and points further north. The road, the port, and the railroad all facilitated the opening of the region to development. In the early 1940s, the Santa Corporation was formed on the model of the Tennessee Valley Authority and charged with regional development. The corporation began expanding the port, and more labor was attracted to the new construction in Chimbote.

In order to house its people, the corporation had to construct housing and to provide school facilities for children as well. An aerial photo of Chimbote at this time reveals that most of the blocks in the town center laid out by Meiggs in the nineteenth century were still largely unoccupied. Efforts of the government to make Chimbote more liveable included draining the malarial swamps that occupied a good deal of the area, constructing a hospital, and beginning a public health service. A public water supply and sewerage system was also designed and started at this time.

At first, the corporation made no serious efforts to control the invasion of the land assigned to it by the government, but in 1952, it tried to force people out of El Acero, a squatter settlement near the port. The major accomplishment of the corporation at this time was the construction of a large hydroelectric plant at Huallanca which was to supply the region with electricity. In order to make good use of the electricity being generated and the coal which had lost its market, it was decided to locate a steel plant at Chimbote, and construction was begun in 1945. Owing to a series of complications, the plant did not finally get into operation until 1958.

Chimbote had always been a fishing port, with most of the fish being sold locally or salted and shipped by railroad to the highlands. Production was small-scale. During World War II, however, there was a considerable demand for fish livers and salted fish. Initially, fishermen brought the fish in on the beach and cut out the livers for sale, leaving the remains. After official objections, they were forced to haul the cut-up fish back to sea for dumping. They quickly realized that there was no need to haul the fish into the port anyway, and began cutting out the livers at sea. As a result of the volume of livers being shipped, people realized that there was a considerable volume of tuna, bonito, and other species available in the area, and the first cannery opened in 1947. Spanish fishermen were brought in to work in this industry, and the fishing industry began to attract people.

The real boom in fishing, however, did not begin until a way of processing *anchoveta* into a more valuable product was discovered. The old system let pelicans, cormorants, and other seabirds feed on the great schools of *anchoveta* right off the coast and deposit their guano on the islands. The guano was then collected for fertilizer. This was a government-assigned monopoly and the basis for the fortune of one of the great oligarchical families in Peru. The first fishermen came from coastal areas, but as the fish-meal industry expanded, people from the highlands moved quickly to go into fishing. The coal business, on the other hand, never recovered from its market loss in World War II, which resulted from mixing good and poor grade coals that fouled equipment in Argentina, its major user.

In 1961, when we first arrived in Chimbote, there were some thirty-five fish-meal and fish-cannery factories in operation, and a steel plant was also making a major smoke contribution to the atmosphere. By that time, Chimbote had grown from a population of about 4,000 in 1940 to 64,000, yet had acquired very few characteristics usually associated with a city. There were numerous factories, considerable traffic congestion, a few multistoried buildings, and one good, large hotel, which had been built by the corporation to attract tourists in earlier days. On the other hand, a number of characteristics normally associated with a city were lacking. The Pan-American Highway and the main street in town were the only paved roads—all the rest were of rough dirt. In addition to the strong smell of the fish factories, the fact that at least three-quarters of the population was without basic services such as electricity, water, and sewers was readily apparent. Trucks, carts, and burros carried water to the houses. Only the old center of town had water, sewerage, and electric facilities. There was no fashionable zone of first-class housing anywhere in the city, the most elegant zone being one of small, wooden prefabricated houses of the corporation in La Calets (Figure 1, Zone C). Enormous areas were covered with straw shacks and poorly made adobe houses. The impression was that of a boom town with newly established factories, temporary

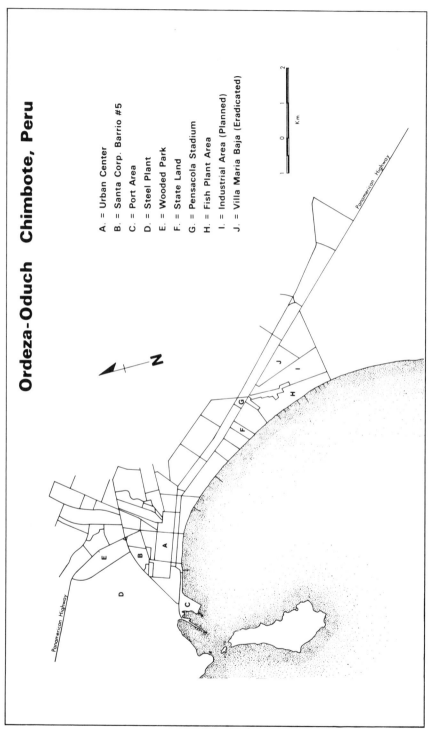

Ordeza-Oduch   Chimbote, Peru

A. = Urban Center
B. = Santa Corp. Barrio #5
C. = Port Area
D. = Steel Plant
E. = Wooded Park
F. = State Land
G. = Pensacola Stadium
H. = Fish Plant Area
I. = Industrial Area (Planned)
J. = Villa Maria Baja (Eradicated)

Figure 1

housing, and a great many bars, restaurants, nightclubs, and bordellos. In this sense, Chimbote resembled many of the famous mining towns which grew from nothing to substantial cities in a very short time.

Many of the people attracted to the city at this time were attracted by the possibility of making a quick fortune. A survey done at this time revealed that most of the population of Chimbote had come within the last ten years, and only 5 percent of the heads of households were natives of the town.[1] Since Chimbote is only about four to five hours north of Lima by road and approximately an hour south of Trujillo, the people who came to Chimbote to make their fortunes did not necessarily live there. People who were obliged to live there, such as the administrators of fish factories or the officials of the Santa Corporation, considered themselves to be on temporary assignment and not permanent residents. Many administrators lived in Chimbote but maintained their families in Lima or Trujillo for the comfort, educational, and health advantages there. A mark of success was replacement as an administrator in Chimbote and reassignment to the principal office in Lima. One of the notable consequences was that very little money was invested in making Chimbote a more desirable place to live. In 1961, Chimbote looked like a small coastal village to which a large number of factories and squatter settlements had been added.

The size and dynamism of the town had by then attracted a large number of migrants, largely from the nearby coast and sierra, but also from Lima. French technicians had been brought in to work on the steel plant, and a number of Peruvians of Italian descent had moved from other places in Peru. In addition to the Spaniards already mentioned, a number of Yugoslavs were attracted to the fishing industry. The Chinese colony in Chimbote continued to grow and prosper with the growth of the town, but most of the Japanese had been removed during World War II. The physical growth pattern outward from the urban center can be seen in Figure 1.

With the incredible population increase during the period from 1940 to 1961, the construction industry also expanded rapidly to become, after the late 1960s, second only to the fishing industry in numbers employed. As long as the population was rapidly expanding, not only were new houses and other buildings needed, but also a large number of people could earn a living by providing goods and services. Therefore, Chimbote experienced a tremendous increase in the number of market stalls, small stores, workshops, street vendors, restaurants, bars, and movies.

Competition for land in Chimbote, which began on a modest scale in 1927 when the indigenous community obtained legal recognition, intensified with the arrival of the Santa Corporation in the 1940s and accelerated with the development of the fishing industry in the 1950s. With the rapid influx of migrants, worthless desert land suddenly acquired value as sites for industry, housing, and business.

Changes in the Social Structure

It is doubtful that any government could have foreseen the explosive expansion that occurred in Chimbote as it multiplied its population from 4,000 in 1940 to 64,000 in 1961 and to approximately 200,000 in 1975. The social structure of the village suffered repeated shocks as new elites arrived in successive waves.

Before World War II, the top of the social structure in the valley was the large landowners, although they spent little time in Chimbote. In Chimbote itself, the upper class consisted of the railroad agent, representatives of the customs agencies and the better-known commercial houses from Lima, the wealthier hotel owners and business people, and political leaders. With the arrival of the Santa Corporation, the first really educated group of professionals, engineers, lawyers, and so forth migrated to Chimbote and settled in at the top of the social structure, displacing most of those who had occupied these prestige positions previously. The old elite was not only displaced, but also ignored by the new elite, as a little colony of outsiders isolated themselves in the corporation housing project, La Caleta, and took control of the town.

If the old elite was shaken by the attitudes and behavior of the corporation officials, it was shattered by the behavior of the migrants who came to work for the corporation, since this group paid them no attention either, did not recognize them as superior, and omitted the traditional obsequious behavior expected from the lower classes. This was not intentional rudeness by the migrants, but an honest estimate of the importance of the old Chimbote elite in the eyes of the newcomers. Moreover, most of the migrants did not originate in the lower classes, so obsequiousness was not part of their normal behavior.

The steel industry brought a very complicated industrial process to the town, requiring large numbers of people in a very complex ordering of skills. Foreign technicians and advisers were needed to supplement the national staff during the first fifteen years or so of the industry's operation. The educational level of administrators and technicians, and their salaries, made them an instant elite.

The development of the fish-meal industry brought a further shock to the social structure. Since this industry was also new to Peru, there were no experienced professionals in the early days to run the plants or the boats. The administrators of the fish-processing plants lacked the educational qualifications possessed by the engineers and lawyers of the Santa Corporation and the steel plant, and therefore were looked down upon and not accepted as part of the real social elite of Chimbote. The fishermen were also looked down upon by the workers of the corporation and the steel plant since they were of inferior educational levels and had no regular income. But when the fishing was good, they were the ones who put money into Chimbote, and commerce quickly developed to meet their needs. The sensibilities of others were shocked when the fishermen did what poor people always seem to do when they strike it rich: they consumed lavishly. Over time, fishing engineers took control of some of the plants, and professional fishermen developed their skills, union institutions, and habits to adjust to the seasonal nature of their industry. By the early 1970s, they had been incorporated into the city as a permanent, integral part of its social structure (Figure 2)

However, one should not conclude that there were no exceptions to this general process. Not all of the mobility of native Chimbotanos into the newer, more complicated system was lateral. Several businessmen were able to rise with the town and remain in the top economic elite; others were not.

Recent Changes which Indicate Maturation in the Urbanization-Industrialization Process

By 1972, a number of indicators pointed to the possibility that the period of most rapid expansion had passed and that a more normal, steady rate of urbanization had begun. Some indicators, however, did not conform to this pattern, the most important of which was the continued population increase. Similarly, the number of people paying business taxes continued to increase with the population, although this may have been a response to the shortage of jobs in major industries, which forced many people into the streets as vendors. On the other hand, by 1968, a number of indicators pointed out that a definite slowdown was in progress. The number of professionals paying the occupational tax showed a marked decline in the rate of increase after 1965 and a leveling-off after 1967. Apparently doctors, lawyers, dentists, and the like were not finding an increasing market for their services.

In general, the major portion of the employment base had not expanded to keep up with the flow of in-migrants, and in some cases it had contracted. The Santa Corporation reached its peak in the number of people employed in 1957 and thereafter declined steadily, finally disappearing altogether in 1975. The steel plant continued to expand but also increased its productivity per man as well as its total production. The corporation and the steel plant together added only 414 new jobs for the entire decade 1960–1970. After the great earthquake of 1970, the steel plant recovered rapidly and continued to expand its labor force to 5,000

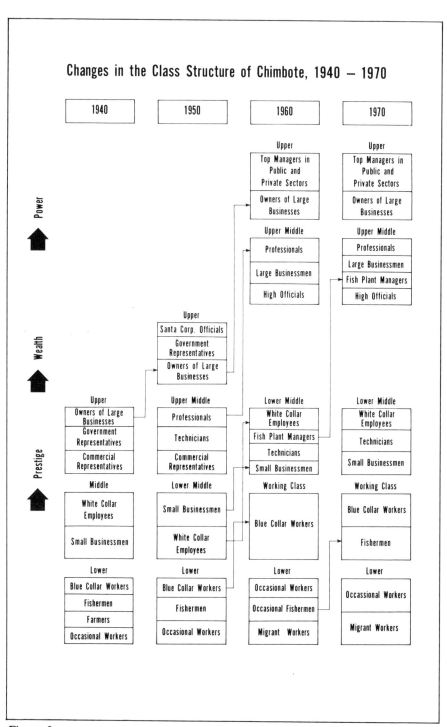

Changes in the Class Structure of Chimbote, 1940 — 1970

Figure 2

by 1975, as compared with 1,500 in 1961. It anticipates further expansion to about 10,000.

The major changes, however, have taken place in the fishing industry, where efficiency increased notably in the 1960s. New controls imposed by both the industry itself and the government limited the size of the catch permitted and controlled the times when people were allowed to fish. This increased efficiency in the fishing process since boats were not permitted to leave port when there were insufficient fish. The fishing industry also increased its efficiency by replacing small boats of 60- to 150-ton capacity with large steel boats of 250 to 350 tons each. The larger boats are more sophisticated and mechanized, but can be handled by the same sized crew as the smaller ones. With fewer boats catching more fish, but with definite limits imposed on the size of the annual catch, fewer fishermen were needed. From a peak of about 5,000 men in 1968, the number of fishermen dropped to about 3,000 in 1975, and it is expected to drop further. At the fish-meal plants, a similar process was under way in the late 1960s as they became more efficient. Both of these changes resulted in a change in the character of the work force. Trained, professional people were required to deal with the more sophisticated equipment.

Two widely used economic indicators, bank deposits and the consumption of electric energy, also show that the boom had ended by 1968. Bank deposits increased with the general prosperity until 1967 and declined through 1972.[2] The consumption of electricity also increased rapidly until 1967; the rate of increase declined during 1968 and became negative thereafter. Its decline has continued since 1968 in all sectors except the steel plant. Similarly, the volume of exports has declined steadily since 1968, and the closing of the fishing industry for the second half of 1972 reduced this even further.

The construction industry was the only major source of employment other than steel which was able to counter this trend; and its continued success relates directly to continued population increase and to the need for reconstruction after the earthquake of 1970. The epicenter of the quake was just offshore from Chimbote and destroyed approximately 80 percent of the city. Suppliers to the construction industry, such as hardware stores and companies supplying cement and other building materials, have all benefited from the reconstruction efforts.

Changes in the Urban Environment since 1961

A number of noteworthy changes have occurred since our first arrival in Chimbote in 1961. The streets in the center of town have all been paved and sidewalks built, making life in the center a good deal more pleasant. These changes, plus the general prosperity of the decade, have permitted many housing improvements in the center. New commercial buildings have been erected and old ones improved. Urban services of water, sewerage, electricity, and garbage collection have been expanded greatly. Housing in the *barriadas*, or "young towns" as they are now called, has continued to improve as people's incomes have permitted them to improve their homes or move to new houses. Similarly, there have been great improvements in the number of schools and recreation facilities and in new housing developments.

Although Chimbote is a town which has been sporadically planned from its onset, it is only recently that authorities have gained increasing control over land use, with the result that the former chaotic patterns of growth have been stopped and planned; orderly growth is now well under way. Successful programs in remodeling squatter settlements have convinced the inhabitants of benefits available through cooperation with the various government agencies. The fish-meal plants, which formerly were scattered along the coast from one end of the city to the other, are now concentrated to the south of the main center of population. Recreational facilities of all sorts have been added to the city—stadiums, an Olympic swimming pool, a park with picnic facilities—and the town has its own professional soccer team. Many of the children of migrants have now grown up and formed families of their own, and these people have loyalties to Chimbote rather than the village or city of their parents.

Since the middle of the 1960s, a private development south of town has been steadily increasing the number of middle- and upper-class families resident in Chimbote. Nevertheless, one of the things that has not changed much over the years is that the principal owners and managers of business and industry in Chimbote still do not live there. Since the revolutionary government has socialized the fishing industry and the government already owned the steel industry, this pattern has simply meant that absentee public officials control Chimbote to a greater extent than was the case before and that the private sector has lost influence. In spite of all of the dramatic improvements in the quality of life in Chimbote which have occurred in the last decade, few of the top managers have settled in Chimbote with their families. In order to understand why this occurs, we shall have to reexamine in greater depth the question of who has settled in Chimbote and why, and look at the institutional basis for the preference to live in Lima on the part of those who hold power in either the private or the public sector.

The Migration Stream to Chimbote

Chimbote has participated in an exaggerated fashion in the same rapid urbanization process that is going on in most parts of the developing world. With the exception of several countries such as Brazil, Ecuador, and Colombia, a high primacy pattern prevails, in which the only city of importance is the capital. Key functions are concentrated in one place, and the country's wealth and power are also concentrated there, with important economies of scale in social overhead facilities. But this leads to the impoverishment of the outlying areas for the benefit of the capital, a process Latin American scholars label internal colonialism. The attractions of the capital city which pull migrants out of the smaller towns and villages include such things as employment opportunities, educational opportunities, health and recreation facilities—all of which make the city an exciting place to live. The capital is where the action is, where the power and influence are; and to take advantage of these benefits, one has to go to the capital.

Who migrates to the city, and how are they different from those who remain in the home village? All migration is selective, but there is no agreement among professionals as to the criteria of selection, except that migrants are normally younger than the general population. Most migrants move to places where they already have relatives who can help them until they are ready to stand on their own feet. Four of five heads of households living in Chimbote in 1962 reported having relatives living in the city. The same survey revealed that although half of the respondents reported that they had been born in small villages or rural areas, only 17 percent had themselves been farmers, and only 39 percent had fathers who had been farmers. A study carried out in the District of Huaylas revealed that after eliminating as many differences as possible between migrants and nonmigrants by interviewing only pairs of brothers, the brother who migrated was the better educated of the two. Small differences in the amount of formal education made considerable difference in the later achievements of these men. One of the more interesting findings of the study was that a man's life chances were also greatly affected by whether he had been raised in the rural area or the town center of the district. Even after an average stay in the cities of twenty years, the men from the town center had not only maintained their socioeconomic advantage over the men from the rural areas, they had in fact increased it.[3]

Migration from rural areas to the cities is not only a result of the attractions of the cities; it is also the result of the pressures of increased population on a fixed land base being worked with a static technology. The natural increase in population for the District of Huaylas for the intercensal period 1941–1961 was 60 percent. Yet the population in 1961 was the same size as twenty years earlier, since all of the increase had migrated, mainly to Lima and secondarily to Chimbote. Out-migration from places such as Huaylas to the cities is disproportionately from the urban part of the district and disproportionately from the middle and upper classes.[4] In order to maintain the same class structure in the district, there has to be a rural-urban migration going on within the district and upward social mobility to fill the slots left by the migrants. Thus, we see the same selective process going on within a small, rural district that we have noted for the nation as a whole, with a constant drain of the best human resources from the smaller to the larger centers. On the international scale, this phenomenon has been labeled the brain drain. It seems to hold true down to the smallest villages.

Consequences of Migration for Places of Origin and Destination

The smaller places pay the costs of raising children to maturity, then the young people leave for the cities before "repaying" the community the costs of their upbringing. The countryside loses the best, in terms of education, that it produces. Those left at home may benefit from remittances of funds from those in the cities and from having relatives in the cities to educate and aid the next group of migrants. Rural areas also benefit from the out-migration since it avoids a decline in the level of living that would otherwise be inevitable with the rising population and static agricultural technology. To the extent that cities can continue to receive excess rural population, pressure on the land does not increase to the point where more intensive agricultural technology is required.[5]

The cities benefit from the selection process for the same reasons that the countryside loses. They receive men of working age with no investment on their part, and they get the best that the countryside has to offer. Migrants who fail to adapt to industrial work or urban life return to the home village, so the city is not burdened with an undue number of misfits. Highlanders are generally eager to lose their identification with the sierra, so cities such as Chimbote do not have large, distinct minority groups or the intergroup hostilities that normally result from such situations. Indeed, Chimbote has been a remarkably cosmopolitan place ever since 1872, when the first Chinese arrived.

If rural-urban migration allows a certain stability in the rural areas, the same cannot be said for the cities. What has been the response of Chimbote's urban institutions to the massive immigration? How do the migrants themselves respond to both the possibilities and the limitations of life in a boom town?

The Power Structure—Local and National

Any local government would be weak in the face of the challenges which have faced Chimbote, but under the Peruvian constitution, local government is especially weak, owing to the high degree of centralization of power in the capital. The city government lacks the right to decide its tax rates, lacks police power to enforce the few dispositions it is allowed to make, and is kept with so few resources that there is very little that it can do to ameliorate the situation. In fact, the annual budget of a single foreign charity in Chimbote is larger than the entire provincial budget. Under these circumstances, it is not surprising that the city has been unable to make adequate provision for such vital services as garbage collection, water, sewerage, and police protection. To make matters worse, Chimbote lost six of its major taxes to the federal government and simultaneously suffered a cut in the federal subsidy to the city for the two-year budget of 1973–1974 and 1975–1976. City services were cut drastically as a result.

Political power is centered in Lima for both the public and private sectors; all decisions of importance are made there. Power in Chimbote, whether in government offices or private companies, is limited to the most minor decisions. If all decisions of importance are made in Lima, it makes sense for the decision-makers to live in Lima. This being the case, it is possible to justify the distrust of local authority and to limit severely its range of action. Local government offices continue to be staffed, but they are relatively powerless to deal with the realities of their city and are dependent upon whatever action is taken by the central government.

The new class structure continues to reflect these old patterns. Those who find themselves obliged to work in Chimbote for the central government or industry generally try to maintain their families in Lima or Trujillo, where life is more comfortable. Decisions affecting the city are made by people with no personal interest in the city. The resident population tends to feel either exploited or ignored by the authorities and lacks the voice to protest. Chimbote has been a place where people have a license to do as they please without having to live with the consequences of their actions. The fish-meal companies were by far the most abusive group in terms of past environmental damage. But they were also the most important contributors of jobs to the community during the boom period.

The absence of the real leaders of Chimbote has meant that there is little interest in improving schools, hospitals, urban services, and so forth on their part, since the temporary residents do not expect to derive the benefits of those services. In recent years, most of the investment in good housing has served to improve housing for the people already there, rather than to encourage government and business leaders to settle permanently in Chimbote. The fact that headquarters are in Lima has led many to believe and to maintain the hope that their assignment to Chimbote is merely temporary, even though some of them have been there for twenty years or more. As a result, those in the public and private sectors who

have the economic and political power needed to bring about improvements in Chimbote are the ones who have the least personal interest in
doing so. Conversely, those who live in Chimbote and cannot expect to
emigrate have the greatest interest in improving the city and are without
the economic and political power to do so.

Old Institutions Inadequate for New Social Problems

One of the traditional obligations of the elite in small towns is to engage in
acts of social concern for the poor. Indeed, it is one of the ways of
validating one's status as upper class. Before World War II, the elite did
have projects, such as providing school uniforms, desks, and nurseries for
poor children. The corporation took over many of these paternalistic
concerns, but the needs soon outgrew its capacities, and by the 1960s,
international agencies arrived on the scene to take over these functions.
The Peace Corps and the U.S. Catholic Church arrived on a noticeable
scale in 1962, and were soon followed by the Foster Parents Plan. In 1961,
a national beer company had to assume the financial and organizational
responsibility for the Fiesta de San Pedro (Chimbote's patron saint) since
no other group could be formed for the purpose. Charity had reached such
a scale that in 1972 a single agency, Foster Parents Plan, served 4,350
families—approximately 26,000 people—in meeting some of their most
urgent needs. The rapid succession of dominant economic interests from
outside, followed by the social work of international institutions, raises
the question, What are the most urgent needs of migrants to Chimbote?

Priorities in Expenditure of Family Income

Migrants to Chimbote typically live with relatives for the period needed to
find a job. This means that they normally move to the most established
areas of the city rather than directly into one of the newer "young towns."[6]
Once they are well connected, they may hear of a planned "invasion" and
sign up to get a lot in the new area. Since many of the people have been
raised without such urban services as running water, sewerage, and
electricity, life in "young towns" is not too difficult to tolerate, especially
since the climate in Chimbote is so mild. The hardships are more than
compensated for by the fact that the lot costs them little and their straw-
mat house is also low-cost and rent-free. Over time, once they feel secure
in their possession of the land and have accumulated a little in savings,
they begin to purchase materials for a more solid house. It normally takes

five to ten years for a newly invaded piece of land to become converted from straw shacks to predominantly permanent housing.

Most of the migrants to Chimbote during its boom period experienced a considerable increase in their level of living. Priority expenditures are food, fuel, and water. After that come medicines and other health-care needs, clothing, transportation, and educational expenses. Housing and furniture occupy a low place in the priority list, so funds not absorbed in the above-mentioned categories are frequently spent on entertainment or electronic gadgets such as radios, record players, tape recorders, TV, and the like, rather than on housing or furniture. About 95 percent of electric appliances are bought on time payments.[7] Since they give immediate gratification and can be paid for rather quickly, these items are more urgently demanded than housing. One should also keep in mind that it is easier to secure credit to buy these things than to guarantee a mortgage, especially if one's income is unstable. In recent years, stable employment has become the rule in the fishing industry, enabling both fishermen and fish-meal factory workers to qualify for mortgages. But population continues to expand far beyond the capacity of the local economy to provide steady jobs.

Available data indicate that the period of remarkably rapid industrial growth of Chimbote has passed, at least for the time being. This should be taken as a relative statement. The vital statistics register still reveals a steady natural increase of approximately 5,000 people per year for the years 1970–1975, plus the number of in-migrants. The economy in general and the fishing industry in particular had lost their ability to provide jobs for the increasing population well before the earthquake of 1970. The earthquake had the effect of masking this condition, since the destruction caused a minor boom in reconstruction which permitted the population to continue increasing in spite of the lack of permanent jobs deriving from a solid economic base. Fortunately, commitments were made by the government before the earthquake to push the industrial development of Chimbote, and since 1972, the steel industry has been accelerating its expansion plans, and several important steel-using industries have been established in Chimbote. The basic social and economic problems of Chimbote derive from the shortage of stable employment opportunities for its citizens. As noted previously, Chimbote has people with the necessary motivation to work, but it lacks people with the political and economic power to direct its development.

Conclusion

In recent years, social scientists in varius disciplines have moved away from treating small population units such as villages as social and cultural units apart from their wider social environment. It is increasingly recognized that we need to consider population units of various sizes in the context of the wider regional, national, and, in fact, world economies and political systems.[8] Authors focusing on conditions in the Third World are arriving at a consensus that the interdependence of these parts of the world with the others led to the development of the industrialized countries and to the underdevelopment of the Third World. This is not to say that the Third World has not undergone development and modernization as a result of its political and economic contacts with the rest of the world, but rather that the rates and directions of development have been different and that the gap between the developed and the underdeveloped countries is growing wider. Moreover, this is seen as a function of the nature of the interrelationships between the industrialized countries and the Third World.

Returning to the interaction of the two major variables under consideration in this volume, population and development, we can see that in the context of a single place and through time, each of these can be viewed as an independent variable "causing" changes in the other. Although our focus has been on one place, Chimbote, we found that we could not understand what was happening there without understanding what was happening in small rural districts nearby, such as Huaylas; nor could we ignore the capital of Peru, Lima, and the larger, less well-defined forces, such as the world market.

The environmental features we found important at various times in the history of Chimbote's development depended upon the existence of the port, the railroad, road transportation, technology, and the world market. As new environmental features were exploited, more opportunities to work and invest appeared, increasing the disparity between Chimbote and the surrounding villages in the region. These greater opportunities to work and invest attracted increasing numbers of people to the port. Increasing employment opportunities in the steel and fish-meal industries in turn attracted many people to provide services for the increasing population, with the result that the growth of the city began to feed upon itself.

Some of the original causal factors in the development of Chimbote are no longer relevant. For example, the railroad, which was of crucial importance to the movement of coal and other minerals from the mountains, was finally destroyed by the earthquake of 1970. Electricity, which was crucial to the starting of the steel industry, is no longer so important to that industry, which has changed processes to more conventional blast furnaces. But once large investments had been made, port facilities developed to handle the necessary traffic, and people settled to work in the plant. Now, the government must not only maintain the plant, but make it larger and more efficient as time goes by. The same phenomenon may be noted with respect to the fishing industry in combination with the steel industry, since the revolutionary government recently transferred the largest shipbuilding company from Callao to Chimbote, where it employs 2,000 workers to build steel fishing boats.

One of the major frustrations at any level of action derives from decision-makers' ability to control only part of the relevant environment. For example, the government has been vigorously controlling anchovy fishing over the past few years in order to ensure a more stable supply. With ownership of the only steel plant and the power to restrict imports of steel, the government can guarantee a market for its steel by requiring other government corporations, such as the boat-building corporation, to buy steel from Chimbote regardless of the price. Similarly, with increasing oil production, in the future the government should be able to control the internal price of oil. But the national government of Peru cannot be expected to control world market prices of fish meal, since it is not the only producer and has no control over the prices of competing products such as soybeans.

At each level of society, there are a number of limiting factors which are completely outside the control of the actors. The peasant cultivator has little, if any, control over the prices of the things that he sells or buys. Major fish-meal producers quickly realized the problems and possibilities of their market and organized a producers' market to drive up world prices. They were partially successful in their efforts at various times, owing not only to their organization, but to the large percentage of the world's fish-meal which came from Peru and the absence of acceptable substitutes. But as is normally the case, the high prices attracted competition from other producers of the same product as well as new substitute products. At the same time, the very high prices and extremely high profitability in the fishing industry led to overproduction in relation to the fish supply. By 1975, the cost of producing fish meal was considerably higher than the price the meal would bring on the world market.

The concepts of colonialsm and internal colonialism, domination, and the like apply at all levels of society—local, regional, national, and international. In his study of Huaylas, Doughty noted a long-term rural-urban rivalry within the district. The rural people felt that the village had disproportionate advantages as the capital of the district. They wanted to split the district and establish a new district capital in the rural area, where they too could enjoy the benefits of national schools and other services now enjoyed only at the district capital.[9] The people in the district capital also felt at a disadvantage in relation to the provincial capital, since the provincial capital is not only larger and located on the main highway, but it enjoys even greater governmental facilities, such as the only high school in the province. People in provincial capitals in isolated areas envy the larger cities, such as Chimbote, and department capitals, such as Hauraz, since these in turn have more to offer. We have noted that the people of Chimbote feel impotent compared to Lima in many areas of activity. Although Lima can and does dominate the rest of the country in a heavy-handed fashion, the intellectuals and politicians of Lima are quick to realize Peru's impotence on the international scene, particularly in relation to the industrialized countries.

We can envision a chain of command, or a chain of "permission," along which the more powerful social units grant permission for or permit development in certain activities, but not others, to the units further down the chain. At each level, people and institutions exploit the possibilities permitted to them and complain about the restrictions imposed upon them. If they feel sufficiently frustrated by the restrictions in their present area relative to what they feel is their potential, they may migrate to the larger, more powerful center, where they feel permitted to exercise a freer range of action. Hence, the brain drain from the rural to the urban part of the district, from the district to the provincial and departmental capitals, from there to the national capital and into the international migration stream. Each higher stratum in this process is able to skim the cream from the lower strata. If the social sciences have any laws which enjoy the power and universality of such laws as the second law of thermodynamics, one would probably be "To those who have, more shall be given."

Notes

* The initial fieldwork in 1961–1962 was carried out as a part of the Cornell-Peru Project (Alan Holmberg, director) and was financed by the National Institute of Mental Health (Research Grant M-5558 and Fellowship No. 5 FLMH-107, 358-02). Subsequent visits to Chimbote were financed by the National Science Foundation Grant to the Pennsylvania State University (1964); the Wenner-Gren Foundation and the Advanced Research Projects Agency (ARPA order 852, Contract No. N00014-67-A-0098-0001) in 1966–1969; Kalamazoo College (1970, 1975); and the United Nations Development Program in 1972.

1. S. Bradfield, "Some Occupational Aspects of Migration," *Economic Development and Cultural Change* 14, no. 1 (October 1965): 61–70.

2. S. Bradfield, "El Proceso de los Cambios Socio-Económicos en Chimbote," in *Esquema General de Desarrollo de Chimbote y su Microregión,* Vol. I, tomo II (Cryrzo-UNDP Planning Project for Reconstruction and Development of Chimbote, 1973), pp. B45–96.

3. S. Bradfield, "Selectivity in Rural-Urban Migration: The Case of Huaylas, Peru," in *Urban Anthropology* A. Southall, ed. (New York: Oxford University Press, 1973).

4. A full ethnographic account of this district is available in Paul L. Doughty, *Huaylas: An Andean District in Search of Progress* (Ithaca, N.Y.: Cornell University Press, 1968).
5. Ester Boserup, *The Condition of Agricultural Growth* (Chicago: Aldine, 1965).
6. For more detailed description of Peruvian squatter settlements, see William Mangin, "Urbanization Case History in Peru," *Agricultural Design* (August 1963); "Latin Ameican Squatter Settlements: A Problem and a Solution," *Latin American Research Review* 2/3 (1967): 65–98; "Squatter Settlements" *Scientific American* (October 1967), 21–29.
7. S. Bradfield, "Migration from Huaylas: A Study of Brothers." (Ph.D. diss., Cornell University, 1963).
8. See, for example, I. S. Barnes, "Class and Committees in a Norwegian Island Parish," *Human Relations* 7, no. 1 (1954): 39–58; Robert A. Manners, "Remittances and the Unit of Analysis in Anthropological Research," *Southwestern Journal of Anthropology* 21, no. 3 (1965): 179–95; André Gunder Frank, *Capitalism and Underdevelopment in Latin America, Historical Studies of Chile and Peru* (New York: Monthly Review Press, 1969); Norman Ashcraft, *Colonialism and Underdevelopment: Processes of Political Economic Change in British Honduras* (New York: Teachers College Press, Columbia University, 1973); Immanuel Wallerstein, *The Modern World-System: Capitalist Agriculture and the Origins of the European World Economy in the Sixteenth Century* (New York: Academic Press, 1974).
9. Doughty, *Huaylas.*

Barry Lentnek

Regional Development and Urbanization in Latin America: The Relationship of National Policy to Spatial Strategies

Latin America is the most urbanized area in the developing world. The role of the urban center in the formation of basic political and economic institutions is profoundly rooted in its cultural history. Even though Latin America was more urbanized than either Africa or Asia at the end of World War II, massive rural-to-urban migration has continued over the past thirty years, so that presently, more than half of all Latin Americans live in urban areas.[1] Yet this phenomenon has occurred without an accompanying increase in material welfare for most people. In fact, it is the urbanization of poverty which has so disturbed observers that they call the process "hyperurbanization."[2]

Here we will examine the governmental policies which have led to massive urbanization in a largely primate pattern. The central thesis is that primate-city development is the result of a mix of national strategies for economic development. These are *national* developmental policies, which suggest a corollary to the thesis: National policy leads to primate-city problems which are essentially *local* and which, because of their national origin, are extremely difficult to deal with on a local level.

Part I examines the basic alternative strategies open to developing nations. Part II presents a brief analysis of the economic history of Latin America. Then spatial strategies for regional and urban development are analyzed with respect to the migration they have generated. Finally, a case is made for a change in basic strategy for the remainder of the twentieth century.

Part I: National Development Strategies

"Development" is at best a complex concept, but its essence is the *improvement through time* of the *economic well-being* of the people of some unit, usually a *nation*. There are severe limits to accomplishing much through redistributing unequally distributed income; thus, basically, we must be concerned with strategies for expanding the national product—increasing the output of goods and services which are available for the consumption of a nation's inhabitants. (Matters of the distribution of these goods and of the time frame in which development is sought are important definitional aspects which are not explored here.)

Five basic strategies may be identified,[3] with emphasis at one extreme on heavy industrialization and emphasis at the other on rural development programs for subsistence farmers. The five are not necessarily mutually exclusive, and they tend to overlap somewhat; but it is also clear that choice must be made. Emphasis cannot be given all five alternatives at once because both economic and human resources are scarce.

The five alternative strategies to be discussed are

1. Heavy industrialization based on natural resource concentrations and oriented eventually to the production of capital goods.
2. Light industrialization with emphasis upon providing consumer goods primarily to the expanding middle classes of the large urban centers. This objective is frequently sought by excluding selected imports (import substitution). Local manufacture presumably has some ripple effect as new industries develop to supply locally produced parts for what may at first be little more than an assembly operation. This process, which moves from assembling foreign produced parts for consumer goods to the development of local suppliers, is referred to as industrializing through backward linkages.
3. Light industrialization with emphasis upon the simplest consumer goods (footware, clothing, food processing, beverages, etc.) and services (basic educational and medical services) and oriented toward market towns and small regional cities.
4. Mechanization and biological modernization of agricultural production, aimed at both increasing domestic food supplies and promoting export agriculture. In some countries, this can be supplemented by heavy investment in mineral production for international markets.
5. Importation of labor-intensive, high-technology manufacturing techniques for producing manufactured goods for the export market. This may be a logical extension of policy 2.

THE HEAVY INDUSTRIALIZATION STRATEGY

Heavy industrialization is based on the transformation of basic mineral resources and is characterized by large size and capital intensity (large investments). Typical heavy industries are steel, petrochemicals, and cement. Before World War II, a primary example of heavy industrialization in Latin America was the steel industry in Monterrey, Mexico.[4] After World War II, Brazil began construction of its Volta Redonda plant; Mexico, which nationalized oil in the 1930s, made heavy investments in its petrochemical complex based on petroleum resources in the northern desert. Puerto Rico built a large petrochemical complex in the early 1960s based on Venezuelan oil and U. S. markets.[5] Venezuela built the celebrated Guayana steel complex based on iron ore resources in the Orinoco River basin.[6] Colombia developed integrated textile production, including textile machinery and basic chemicals and dyes, as well as some refining capacity for domestic oil consumption and a small steel complex, again for national markets. Refining of copper and tin in Chile and Bolivia remained in foreign hands; facilities for producing aluminum from Jamaican bauxite are located in the United States, and refining of Venezuelan crude oil is still primarily done overseas. While Argentina installed considerable machinery and automotive assembling capacity around Buenos Aires and Córdoba in the late 1940s and early 1950s, it never has completed an iron-steel-machinery complex owing to lack of domestic raw materials and a large-enough market.

Heavy industry requires the importation of large amounts of very expensive capital equipment over an extended length of time. Thus, the strain upon foreign currency reserves is severe. It usually also depends upon the presence of one or more raw materials sufficiently concentrated so as to be economically exploitable. The capital-intensive character of heavy industry implies employment of relatively few workers per unit of investment and per unit of output. Frequently implied also are large investments in expensive overhead capital such as railroad and road networks, electricity supplies, and waste-disposal systems. Such investments are usually expected to be governmentally provided. In addition, heavy investment in human resources is usually required to provide the skilled labor, technical, and managerial staffs of major industries.

Development via heavy industrialization has some necessary policy implications.[7] First, large proportions of current and future foreign earnings must be set aside in order to acquire the necessary foreign equipment, technology, and personnel. In the absence of such earnings, explicit borrowing abroad or permission of foreign investment (implicit borrowing) is necessary. Second, domestic consumption may be postponed for long periods, as heavy industry usually produces only intermediate goods and certainly has a long gestation period. Third, large investments are concentrated in small regions for long periods of time. These favored regions receive the direct benefits of the investment (e.g., wages paid for plant construction). They also receive in exaggerated form the benefits of the multiplier and accelerator effects (i.e., "snowball" effects) familiar to students of elementary economics. These tend to be exaggerated because the lack of integration (another definition of "underdeveloped") prevents rapid dispersion of the multiplier-accelerator effects through the whole national economy. This may be very inflationary, which, coupled with the postponement needs, the nonconsumable nature of increased imports, and the need for heavy social overhead capital, suggests heavy inflationary pressures as characteristic of this approach. Finally, heavy industrialization, as noted above, tends to generate long-term inequalities in relative growth rates between regions and thus significant long-term migration flows. This aspect will be discussed in more detail as a part of spatial strategies for development.

Heavy industry is characterized by large economies of scale, that is, a large capital investment to be recovered by spreading it over a very large output. This implies large markets, with market size being a function of both the population and the average income (and its distribution). Only large (Brazil, Argentina, etc.) and/or wealthy (Venezuela) countries can expect to have markets of sufficient size to support heavy industry. Parenthetically, it is this very feature of industrialization which provides major impetus to expand market size through international economic integration (e.g., LAFTA). Finally, governments desiring to follow this route must be able to cope with the political strains inherent in the process of diverting large proportions of national resources to relatively small regions of the country.

THE URBAN MIDDLE-CLASS CONSUMER-GOODS STRATEGY

The most widely pursued strategy for development in Latin America has centered upon the following chain of interlinked policies. First, policies are promulgated to prevent or to limit importation of light consumer goods (e.g., clothing, textiles, white goods, electrical appliances).[8] Next, capital and technology are imported for the purpose of domestic assembly or manufacture of the items in question (actually, these steps are often reversed in practice). Third, the industry goes through a shakedown period when difficulties in achieving a smooth production flow are resolved and a domestic labor force is trained. Fourth, technical and managerial staffs are gradually trained to replace foreigners.

There is no logical limit to which this import substitution industrialization (ISI) may be carried. It starts with the simpler, lighter goods and *may* eventually be carried further to include capital goods and the products of heavy industry. In any case, a ripple or multiplier (not income) effect through the economy is expected through time as both forward (service) and backward (parts-supplier) linkages develop.

As a national strategy, ISI tends to distinctive results with respect to location, specifically in reinforcing urban primacy. First, almost by definition, the products selected are either of sophisticated and expensive processes or of limited appeal since they are *not* produced locally. With ISI, the local inputs (capital, entrepreneurial capacity, skilled labor) are most likely to be found in the primary city—and so is the market. So the import-substituting industries are likely to locate near both their inputs and their markets, contributing directly and indirectly (through the income multiplier and accelerator effect) to regional inequalities.[9]

Two corollary policies may exacerbate the regional disparities. Financing for this general policy may come from increased taxes, and a likely source is increased taxes on exports, usually agricultural or mineral products. Further, as industry becomes increasingly important, political pressures will be strong to keep the prices of food down (as one feature of policies to keep wages down and labor unrest at a minimum). Both policies, likely but not necessary corollaries of ISI, favor the urban sector over the rural (raw materials-exporting) sector. The result may be rapid growth of gross national product (GNP) and increasing income inequality between regions and urban and rural areas.[10] This accelerates growth in metropolitan areas, concentrates attention upon the school system which produces skills useful in metropolitan areas, and leads to massive rural-to-urban migration. Another possible consequence is overconstruction of plant and equipment for the production of consumer goods purchased by only a minority of the population.

Since the process involves deliberate inequality in intranational growth rates in income and employment, the phenomenon of primacy is not a surprising outcome. Income-earning differentials and changes in them are prime motivations for immigration; policies which increase motivations for immigration; policies which increase already existing differentials can be expected to accelerate migration.

THE RURALIST AGRICULTURAL STRATEGY

This alternative puts secondary emphasis on the national rate of growth and primary emphasis on improving food production at the grass roots— the subsistence farm where poverty is located. It consists of a set of policies to improve knowledge, production, and marketing efficiency for traditional agriculture. An integral part of this strategy is a comprehensive revision of the traditional roles which govern the relationship of farm labor and the land. It is not possible to discuss here all the ramifications of agrarian reform; basically, it involves an institutional revolution which gives the person a stake in the land he farms and a direct and clear relationship between his labor and investment and his income. In addition to rewriting the rules regarding land tenure, the whole of the agricultural infrastructure is involved—transportation and marketing, education and extension, credit, technology and the availability of appropriate technology. This strategy envisages fundamental transformation of most of the agricultural sector, in which there are myriads of participants to be reached, convinced, trained. It is necessarily comprehensive, slow, and requires great administrative skill and patience.

The effective pursuit of this strategy can result in a substantial increase in national standards of living, a fall in urban food prices, and the diversification of agricultural exports. Probably agrarian reform will increase the demand for machinery import and increase the use of petroleum for fuel, fertilizer, and transportation. Improved grass-roots agriculture will not necessarily increase agricultural exports Thus, the net effect may be (temporarily) increased dependence abroad, subjecting the balance of payments to the effects of a shift in the terms of trade against raw-materials producers. This is a key long-term relationship in the theoretical contructs of some development economists.

For reasons of justice, ruralist strategies are often advocated by idealistic leftists both in the United States and in Latin America.[11] This policy has rarely been pursued, however, for any appreciable length of time by Latin American governments because it approaches development primarily at the level of the politically impotent peasant, involves great losses for the politically powerful landowners, and does little initially for the urban middle classes who are beginning to exercise political clout. Cuba pursued a ruralist strategy after the failure of Castro's version of the Great Leap Forward (i.e., heavy industry in a short period of time) during the period 1960–1963.[12] A ruralist strategy based on sugar was avidly pursued during 1964–1970 and then abandoned in favor of a mixed agricultural-industrial regional development strategy, to be discussed below. Costa Rica followed an essentially ruralist strategy for a considerable period of time until the early 1970s, when the emphasis shifted toward urban middle-class goods orientation. This occurred because of a shortage of arable land and the growing opportunities in the Central American Common Market.[13]

The mechanism of the ruralist strategy is to create at the base of the social pyramid a more productive class among the very poor. This group will begin to produce marketable surpluses demanding the evolution of forward linkages in the form of marketing, storage, transport, and even manufacturing facilities. As the surplus evolves, there will also be backward linkages in the form of simple machine manufacture and distribution, distributing points for agricultural services, and information. The demands for these linkages arise in geographic dispersion, and one would expect, then, that considerable emphasis would evolve around the small, decentralized, urban-rural service centers as opposed to the primate city. In other words, this strategy envisages growth impetus coming from the widely dispersed small producer.

Mexico has recently embarked on such a strategy to a limited extent (about 20 percent of current capital investment) because of an accumulation of problems inherited from the previous emphasis upon urbanization and industrialization.[14] Since this has occurred only since 1973, it is still too early to evaluate the results. Ruralist strategies are, however, very *de modo* in present hemispheric discussions of development strategies and problems. Note that ruralist strategies implicitly deny the efficacy of the "trickle down" or "trickle out" expectations of some other strategies.

REGIONAL DEVELOPMENT STRATEGIES

The above-mentioned development strategies are based on economic sectors—that is, heavy industry, consumer-goods industry, and agriculture—and each has different spatial implications. Another approach is regional and addresses the issue of *where* to develop before asking *what* to develop. That is, the first step is a clear designation of the regions within a nation which are to be developed by exploiting locally available economic potentials. Well-known advocates of this basically different approach toward the formulation of national development strategies are J. Friedmann,[15] A. Kuklinski,[16] N. Hansen,[17] and E. A. J. Johnson.[18] The Cauca Valley Corporation in Colombia, dating from the 1950s and taking its cues from the Tennessee Valley Authority (TVA), is an example. In Brazil, great emphasis has been given to development in the northeast and in the Amazon, not so much because of their great potentialities, but because of the great poverty compared to other regions.

There are two types of general regional development strategies which have been advocated in the literature. The first is the regionally concentrated decentralization strategy pioneered by the French regional economists and touted under the labels growth-pole and growth-center development. Besides in France itself, this strategy has been followed to varying degrees of both consistency and success in Poland[19] and the People's Republic of China.[20] The central motive of this strategy is the "integration" of national space by heavy investment in regional industrial centers which are supposed to serve as an "*industre mortice*"[21] or "*armature urbain*"[22] for the national economy. These centers are supposed to be the foci upon which transport systems converge, the centers for transmission of contemporary urban social and economic values (via hierarchic elements of higher education, control over telecommunications, local headquarters for modernization agencies such as development banks, and extension services), and the places from which capital and labor are mobilized to increase both industrial and agricultural production. The role of these centers in the national sectoral investment strategies is not specified, and various authors view it differently. Nonetheless, these places are considered basically as new locations for accumulations of industries which might otherwise have located in primate cities.

In the Latin American context, growth-center theory essentially is based on an expectation that the urban middle-class consumer-goods industry strategy will be pursued, albeit in a number of regional cities. In other words, the growth-center strategy is a special case of the national development strategy based upon expanded output of consumer goods for the urban middle class.[23]

A different type of regional development strategy is advocated for the Republic of India by E. A. J. Johnson.[24] He notes that underdeveloped economies have few small market centers compared to the large number of such centers in developed economies. He argues that these centers are links between masses of rural peasantry and the industrial elements of the national economy and are conduits for the transmission of modernizing ideas downward and market information upward. Thus, governments should deliberately foster the creation and the expansion of numerous small towns to provide articulation points within the rural economy.

This strategy is basically ruralist, but urban in locational context. It differs from growth-center strategy in that the production goals focus upon provision of modern inputs, technical information, and marketing-storage facilities, all of which are aimed at modernizing agriculture and raising rural incomes. These centers are essentially different from the growth centers or poles discussed previously. These are decentralized to bring about a modernization and commercialization of *agriculture*. The poles, on the other hand, are to provide dispersion for industry, largely to satisfy the needs of middle-class consumer-goods demands. The ideas are very different.

EXPORT OF MANUFACTURED GOODS STRATEGY

The last strategy for development is quite recent in origin and involves the emergence in Latin America of a new stage of underdevelopment (i.e., a Third World of intermediate or semi-development as opposed to a Fourth World of very poor, still predominantly rural national economies). Specifically, Argentina, Brazil, Colombia, Mexico, and Venezuela all have well-developed industrial plants producing respectable quantities of steel, petrochemicals, machinery, and electrical goods. It is natural that they would turn to these industries as potential earners of foreign exchange, particularly in the face of severe balance-of-payments pressures caused particularly by increased oil import prices. Balance-of-payments pressures have become increasingly serious with ISI successes since import lists have changed from luxury goods for consumption to the raw materials and capital goods on which the new industry feeds—and the absence of which leads to decreases in employment and incomes, with negative multiplier effects. Thus, minimizing balance-of-payment pressures by series of policies to encourage exports—of manufactures or not—is an entirely understandable approach.

If there is substantial excess industrial capacity (which does tend to occur, for reasons not to be discussed here), three sets of markets exist to help utilize capacity: (a) various policies to expand local consumption (subsidies, reduced taxes, elimination of foreign competitors or near-competitors); (b) formation of trading partnerships with neighbors (common markets), which gives larger markets for some commodities, but also, in reciprocation, increases competition in others; and (c) encouragement of expanded exports to nonneighboring countries (export subsidies, political pressures in the developed nations, etc.). There is, of course, no reason why all three should not be pursued simultaneously.

Each strategy has distinctive problems. Enlarging domestic demand in rural areas requires onerous political decisions concerning decentralization of investment and changes in the sectoral pattern of investment, from creating capacity to producing sophisticated consumer goods and toward investment in agricultural-producers goods and rural infrastructure. Most difficult, it requires a national incomes policy that favors the farmer and the marginal urbanite at the expense of the urban middle class and the ruling elite.

The key difficulty in pursuing a common-market strategy is the distribution of production rights for the various products among the member countries. The Central American Common Market, the Andean Compact, and LAFTA itself constantly deal with this issue. And there is an impressive number of other nontrivial technical problems in the formation of an effective common market. A few examples are the settling of trade imbalances, coordination of monetary and fiscal policies, and the creation of regional transport and power systems. The process is long and complex, with new problems arising as some are settled.

Finally, the prospects for shipping large quantities of manufactured goods to North American and European markets are dim. The growing volume of Mexican exports to the U. S. market and continued high unemployment in the United States have kept the Congress nervously eyeing competitive imports from whatever source. Balance-of-payments pressures, because of the oil crisis, reinforce the tendency to regard imports with a jaundiced eye. Europeans have always pursued far more restrictive policies toward the importation of unfinished goods than has the United States. Thus, it is unlikely that the developed world will allow Latin American countries to expand manufactured exports by significant amounts without complex and expensive reciprocal actions. Export-based strategies for expansion of industrial goods will tend toward a continuation of primate-city patterns, with a possible emphasis upon the old coastline cities. There may be some acceleration in the growth of large regional industrial centers based on raw-material proximity.

Before considering regional and urban options in the light of alternative national strategies for development, it is necessary to consider the Latin American historical tradition of urbanization.

Part II: Historical Perspective on
Latin American Urbanization Patterns

One distressing tendency in the regional economic development literature is that authors make policy recommendations on the basis of their own value systems without taking Latin American-held values into account and without making either set of values explicit. Most of the argument on policy concerning hyperurbanization stems from differences among authors in their perceptions of the desired means toward the end of creating a hierarchy of urban centers. This section considers the historic pattern of urbanization in Latin America and follows this with comments on the values among Latin American elites today. We can then turn to an analysis of national development strategies based on socially held values and the resultant urbanization patterns.[25]

Urban places in Latin America were founded for radically different purposes than were most urban centers in either Anglo-American or Europe. From the very beginning, Latin American cities were meant to serve as the organizing and colonizing centers for empire. Richard Morse describes the social-political pattern characteristic of the Latin American colonial city as "patrimonial."[26] Essentially, most towns were governed by *caciques* and informal councils of landed gentry who dominated the surrounding countryside by means of their control of the land. These patterns of settlement and land use remain today the dominant feature of the spatial organization of Latin American societies.

Subsequent to independence in the early nineteenth century, there was a period of strong regionalism established by self-assertive urban regions seeking a degree of independence from the central governments. The political struggle between federalists and centralists was a struggle for power between the elites of the national capitals and the elites of the regional centers. Centralists eventually won the struggle, largely because of the dynamism of the export sectors and the income, power, and functions related thereto. National capitals reflected this in rapid growth and importance; in most countries, they became primate cities in wealth and income by the 1920s. Government bureaucracies grew rapidly, and national and international financial institutions located their principal offices in the seats of power. Income and population grew large enough to encourage light industry in the immediate vicinity. Agriculture, too, had to adjust to provide the demands of the city for food, especially perishables.[27]

The collapse of international markets in the 1930s put severe strains on the primate city, one of the functions of which was to service the international markets. One response was to turn existing resources to manufacturing substitutes for imports no longer available as supplies of foreign exchange disappeared. This is the ISI referred to earlier, and it contributed to the existence of the primate city.[28]

There were some efforts by some of the larger countries to undertake heavy industry even before the Great Depression. Examples are the Torcuato di Tella steel and automobile complex in Argentina[29] and the steel industry in Monterrey, Mexico. Similar strategies with other products were the textile industries in Antióquia, Colombia; São Paulo, Brazil; and Mexico City. Massive investment in heavy industry did not preclude utilization of the import substitution strategy at the same time, as in the case of post-World War II Brazilian steel production and the Mexican investment in petrochemicals. In fact, heavy industry is really just a special case of ISI.

National development planning became a conscious effort only after World War II for virtually all of Latin America, with the notable exception of Mexico, which initiated planning in the 1920s. Probably the most spectacularly successful effort at planned regional development was the Guayana steel industry complex in Venezuela.[30] The most spectacularly unsuccessful efforts at planned regional development were the Peronista effort at forced heavy industrialization in Argentina in the 1940s and early 1950s and Castro's effort at forced heavy industrialization in Cuba in the 1960s.

SUMMARY OF HISTORICAL ANALYSIS

Twentieth-century elites have in large part determined the pattern of urbanization in Latin America by their choices of national development strategies. To view this pattern as a result of spontaneous innovation or of economies of scale resulting from maximizing economic behavior is to fail to understand the essence of Latin American culture and society.[31] On the other hand, imagining a nostalgic desire for a rural yeomanry and a rurally oriented, service-based, central-place hierarchy is equally at variance with reality. These societies have been based on the territorially aggrandizing, urban-centered hierarchy of political power, at least since the conquistadores—if not before.

If this interpretation is correct, most Latin American governments are committed to a long-run policy of supporting and expanding a hierarchically organized set of urban middle-class populations. Short of a profound shift in power, these sets of values are likely to dominate investment decision-making in the foreseeable future. The vast literature dealing with the truly awe-inspiring scope of rural-to-urban migration is a testament to the nearly universal perception by rural folk in Latin America that the future lies in the centers of national power.

Part III:
Spatial Development Strategies

Most regional development specialists are actively concerned with the promotion of decentralized investment activities. Their writing includes hand-wringing over the current policies, which are centripetal to the great urban centers, and attempts to demonstrate the benefits of investments outside the central cities. Most Latin Americanist geographers believe in the social, moral, and ecological values of decentralized settlement patterns. This may seem peculiar if it is supposed they are sensitive to the cultural values of the region. Their policy conclusions are distinctly un-Latin American because they favor some form of decentralization policy and differ only with respect to the appropriate degree.

The remainder of this section will examine alternative regional strategies which are consistent with Latin American practices previously described, in light of scholarly preferences for decentralization. Alternatives will also be explored. This has some obvious advantages. First, we can examine policy on its own merits, without concern for political considerations. Second, specific attention to the spatial and human implications is a fresh approach to economic and technical decisions.

RESOURCE-BASED REGIONAL INDUSTRIAL DEVELOPMENT

Most regional resource-based economic models begin with the discovery of a natural resource for which an external market exists. The problem then concerns the scheduling and financial requirements of "developing" or exploiting this resource, providing a transport link to external markets, and making sure that the necessary infrastructure is provided. The latter includes secondary transportation, urban housing for staff and workers, needed power supply, and ancillary social services. The project is evaluated in terms of return on investment, impact on employment, and, usually, implications for foreign trade and balance of payments. The World Bank and the major sources of bilateral investment banking frequently undertake such analyses.[32] Regional scientists, economists, and planners examine projections of income and employment to assure that bottlenecks are foreseen and minimized. These projects frequently involve low labor-output and labor-capital ratios and create a small and well-paid industrial work force in the midst of a mass of poorly paid people whom the World Bank considers to be employed in the "informal sector."[33]

Depending on the industry and the level of national demand for industrial products, subsequent investment is devoted to further elaboration of the materials obtained from the primary industry. A. O. Hirschman[34] has made the most perceptive comments on these forward linkages. These projects tend to require massive amounts of foreign exchange and to have long periods of gestation, i.e., the investment is large and the payoff slow. With respect to the foreign-exchange requirement, there are few sources: (a) increased exports or increased taxes on current foreign-exchange earnings, (b) reduced imports, or (c) borrowing abroad. In any case, the result is a diversion of resources from all parts of the country to the favored region.

Another aspect of the project-oriented, natural-resource-based regional policy is that it eventually entails modernization of surrounding agriculture in order to provide perishable foodstuffs to the urban-industrial labor force. Furthermore, as Mamalakis has demonstrated so well,[35] once an industrial region emerges, its leadership tends to influence the national government in the direction of cumulative investment in the same region. In short, industrial regions, once established, demonstrate remarkable persistence in the direction of further growth.

URBAN-BASED CONSUMER-GOODS DEVELOPMENT

Urban-based consumer-goods development implies the industrial labor force is concentrated in a few city regions, because the industries are market-oriented and their economic base is government employees and related ancillary services. Income concentration, including income transfer to one, two, or three major cities, is expected for considerable periods of time. To ascribe the motivaton for industrial location to "innovative sources" is to assume that the governmental and industrial bureaucracies contain a disproportionate share of the innovative talent of a nation. But the chain of causality leading from power to population concentration in space is more than sufficient to account for regional concentration of development without resort to debatable spatial concentration of innovative talent.[36]

If this interpretation is correct, new growth poles will occur if and only if there is a shift of political power away from the primate city, by violent or peaceful means. Political analysis of natural power and priority structures lies outside the scope of this chapter, but a major conclusion is that the geographic distribution of city sizes remains primate at various spatial scales so long as government policy seeks to supply the urban middle class with durable consumer goods and modern services.[37] A striking example is the SUDENE regional development program in northeast Brazil.[38] After decades of attack on the problem of poverty in the northeast, the initial result was the ascension of two *regional* central cities, Recife and Salvador.

John Friedmann has outlined this policy in *Urbanization, Planning, and National Development*.[39] He ascribes the principal cause of primacy to the spatial concentration of innovations, political power, and markets as well as to urban economies of scale. As Friedmann sees it, primate cities attract innovative personalities by providing a social setting within which innovation is encouraged. Thus, primate cities are the first locations in which new goods, techniques, and organizations appear. These innovations then spread throughout the periphery in a pattern of hierarchical diffusion.[40] Hence, the core always has a monopoly over innovative economic behavior and therefore earns monopoly profits in the Schumpeterian sense. When this is combined with associated location factors such as market concentration and economies of scale, the reason modernization proceeds from core to periphery is clear. What is not at all clear is either how a nation develops an innovative core in the first place or how a nation develops secondary growth centers or cores given an original national center.

Friedmann's policy prescriptions largely deal with the problem of deliberate development of secondary growth centers. Unfortunately, his suggestions involve little more than a regional variant of Rosenstein-Rodan's "big push," in which appreciable investment resources are dispersed in a single locale so that an investment threshold is crossed which will (presumably) be self-feeding.[41] The problem, of course, is that the "big push" is probably insufficiently large to be carried out simultaneously in several locales; thus, it is likely to reinforce the primate city or to favor only one of several deserving secondary centers.

Most industry in Latin America is already underutilized owing to (a) insufficient internal markets, and (b) scale appropriate for larger or richer countries. Relocating plants in secondary centers does not solve this excess capacity problem. If the national market for finished goods and the location of intermediate-goods producers are already around the primate city, location of additional capacity elsewhere is an uneconomic proposition, except as the economy may eventually grow to utilize the capacity. It is little wonder that managers of large producing concerns have shown a great reluctance to decentralize. While Friedmann's criticism of plant location bias toward the site of raw materials is well taken, his growth-center theory leads to the expectation of nearly total spatial concentration in a handful of large metropolises and also to the conclusion that decentralization policies are neither feasible nor wise from the viewpoint of maximum growth in GNP! The consequences for migration patterns are obvious.

AGRARIAN-BASED POLICY OF RURAL DEVELOPMENT

This policy is based on a combination of political reform of land-tenure systems and deliberate stimulation of food and fiber production. The proponents of rural development strategies fall into two major ideological groups. The first group is the political radicals of the Left such as André Gunder Frank, who see the urban middle-class populations as essentially parasitic with respect to their country brethren.[42] They use "internal colonialism" to describe a two-step relationship in which the bourgeoisie—the radical term for the urban middle class—is economically exploited by foreign metropolitan governments and multinational corporations. The first step involves several aspects: (a) urban middle-class people constitute markets for the products of capitalistic industrial nations; (b) the bourgeoisie is the matrix from which multinational corporations earn large profits, to be expatriated; (c) the urban middle class, by its dominance over national economic life, controls the exports of primary goods to the Western world. The second step in the radical model is the Latin American bourgeoisie's exploitation of the country's natural resources in order to support its own life-style—essentially copied from abroad. It is this last relationship that is referred to as internal or neocolonialism.

To break this two-step exploitation, radicals argue for a number of interrelated programs. Some of the most common aspects of this program are

1. Nationalization of foreign holdings throughout the country.
2. A thorough land reform which essentially removes absentee landlords and moneylenders from the countryside.

3. Massive investment in rural social overhead capital (roads, dams, schools, health facilities, and improved production technology).
4. Focus of urban investment upon small service centers in rural towns.
5. Focus in large cities upon production for internal consumption of low-priced, common consumer goods.
6. Sometimes, a concurrent policy of fostering heavy investment in basic industry, although this will depend upon geographic and economic circumstances.[43]

The effect of these policies is to decentralize population growth and to promote greater equalization of interregional income. Apparently in Cuba and also in radically Left regimes outside of Latin America, there is a deliberate effort to discourage people from migrating to the national capital.

A second group of advocates of rurally oriented development policies is actually conservative in its political philosophy. Its objectives of a decentralized population and more equal income distribution are those held by the radicals, but policies differ. This group extols the virtues of a more "natural" existence which, it is hoped, preserves the cultural heritage of the small towns and villages. Colonization schemes, moderate land reform, and adoption of intermediate technology are general policies. The viewpoint and methods of this group are easily found in the land-reform provisions of the Alliance for Progress documents generated from the Punta del Este, Uruguay, conference of 1961.[44] Numerous articles describe various aspects of land reform and its relationship to the modernization of agricultural production in Latin America throughout the 1960s.[45] The problem with this conservative strategy is that a serious diversion of national income away from the large cities is necessary to make the policy effective. How this is to be accomplished without a great deal of government control never has been clear.[46]

There is accumulating evidence of the difficulties of pursuing a policy of backward integration from a consumer-goods industry servicing a small urban middle class. Bolivia, Peru, and to a more moderate extent Mexico are endeavoring to attempt one variant or another of the ruralist strategy. Part of the motivation is spatial social justice. A major motivation, however, is the need to expand domestic markets so as to absorb present excess industrial capacity. This shift in policy toward the development of rural markets for consumer goods has profound implications for regional development.

The last spatial strategy to be discussed presumes that a shift toward a more dispersed market for consumer goods (with obvious consequences for intermediate and primary industrial output) will occur for essentially political reasons.

There are two approaches toward the development of urban places outside of those expanding metropolitan-dominated core areas. One is the familiar growth center, touted so often in the regional development literature. This is a rather large city distant enough from the primate metropolis to nurture its own extensive hinterland.[47] The initial population sizes of these centers are often in the 50,000 to 250,000 range, and these cities provide a wide variety of commercial, banking, and local government functions along with some food-processing and other light consumer-goods industries. The purpose of designating the regional city as a growth center is to foster the rapid diversion of industrial growth from the national metropolis to the regional city and thus assure large external economies of scale. Rapid industrial growth of the regional center is to create a local market for surrounding agricultural production, to serve as a point for the transmission of urban values and life-style, and in general to be a catalytic element in the modernization of the surrounding regional hinterlands.

The principal motivations in diverting growth from the metropolis to the regional center are varied and are given different emphases by different authors:

1. Avoidance of diseconomies of scale associated with further growth in the metropolitan region.
2. Diffusion of modernizing forces by the deliberate growth of new points from which innovative ideas may spread.
3. Reversal of spatial inequalities in economic and social welfare created by too great a concentration of investment in a few centers.
4. Creation of new opportunities for mobilization of local talents, capital, and raw materials.
5. Provision of intermediate-sized places to serve as intervening opportunities for rural-to-urban migrants, thus reducing the presumed shock of direct transplantation of rural folk into the metropolis.[48]

The consensus of opinion is that diffusion of urban growth in national geographic space will save scarce capital and promote the equalization of economic opportunities.

The desire to establish new plants away from the center implies the need for industrial expansion. But most Latin American industries suffer from excess capacity, so that the incentives for creation of large amounts of new plant and equipment are weak. Furthermore, the locus of demands is the metropolitan core. Unless this changes, or unless there are compensating advantages to location away from the center, industry is not likely to locate in eccentric locations. As a result, virtually all growth-center plans involve a combination of positive incentives for away-from center location and penalties for in-center locations in order to make the policy of decentralization work.

Positive incentives involve the construction of industrial parks, the improvement of high-speed, high-capacity trunk lines to the metropolitan core, tax rebates for new investment which are tied to geographic locations in the regional centers, deliberate excess capacity in utility services in advance of industrial location, improvements in telecommunications, and favorable terms for importation of capital goods.[49] All of this can be expensive. The costs of providing the necessary infrastructure and financial incentives in a regional center are likely to be substantially higher than those of similar new investment in the metropolitan core. Furthermore, these positive incentives are often not enough—for example, note the French and Mexican experiences.[50] So proponents of growth centers may need to resort to economic sanctions. Some of the more obvious possibilities are

1. Limiting the extension of utilities in the metropolitan area.
2. Forcing industries to absorb a larger share of the tax burden of the metropolitan area.
3. Restricting import licenses for creation of new plant and equipment in the core region.
4. Prohibition of new industrial growth in the primate city.

Most of these measures simply increase the cost of providing goods in the metropolis. If firms locate in the core region anyway because of the influence of other location factors, firms are likely to pass most of the additional costs on to the consumer, reducing output and employment as sales decrease.

The proponents of growth-center strategies argue that short-run economic rationality can lead to long-run economic nonsense because the successful creation of new growth centers will ultimately generate the same conditions which initially made the metropolitan center so attractive to industrialists. This is a novel application of Say's Law, which can be paraphrased as "production creates its own demand."[51] And growth-center theorists end up advocating a regional variant of Rosenstein-Rodan's policy of the "big push." It is not mere coincidence that growth-center strategies are so frequently found in command economies where massive spatial transfers of capital away from metropolitan centers are managerially feasible.

Growth-center strategies are attractive because they preserve the urban middle-classs focus underlying the development planning of most Latin American countries. They are unattractive to some degree because decentralization runs across the grain of the hierarchic traditions of the government and managerial bureaucracies. To the extent that growth poles or growth-center ideas have become part of the public debate, the partisans of the growth-center concept depend for their support upon regional economic elites concentrated in urban areas.

Perhaps the major fault of the arguments related to growth-pole or growth-center theory lies in the notion, seldom made explicit, that development will occur from the top down in a strict hierarchy of urbanized regions. Welfare is usually visualized as trickling down. Progress, it is assumed, must emanate from the great urban places.

Concentration on primate development results in small geographic markets in the center and little market development in the hinterlands. The small national markets encourage the development of international markets, at times with considerable subsidization and frequently at the cost of considerable instability. Finally, the great disparities in levels of income, reinforced by different roles of growth, may cause increased internal stresses.

The alternative form of regional development is based on the proliferation of commercial towns and small cities. Agriculture is not the primary focus of investment; nonetheless, central-place-type regional schemes depend upon successful modernization of farming practices. This approach has been argued most persuasively by E. A. J. Johnson in his book *The Organization of Space in Developing Countries.*[52] The essence is to contrive market systems which will release the productivity of peasant villages from the bonds of interlocked and socially sanctioned institutional arrangements, such as (a) lack of accessible outlets for farm produce, (b) inadequate and usurious farm credit to peasants, (c) poor transport infrastructures which depresses the farmgate product prices and raises input costs, (d) lack of communication concerning production technology and market conditions; and (e) unstable prices without governmental supports and/or monopolistic purchasing arrangements by agricultural crop purchasers.

Johnson argues that large numbers of high-density towns can serve as a catalytic element in dramatically increasing productivity in the countryside. If this is true, a side effect will be that of drastically reduced costs of living in those smaller cities. This *may* mean lower-cost labor. (There is no necessary direct relationship between either cost-of-living differentials and wage differentials or money-wage levels and labor costs.) Increased agricultural productivity will also increase the demands of farmers for light industrial goods—which may also encourage the establishment of industry away from the central city.[53]

Pursuing a regional development strategy focused on the elements of urban hierarchies is appealing. Latin American economies have reached a stage where much pent-up or latent domestic demand for light consumer goods can be met by utilizing existing plant and equipment in urban centers. This serves to lower average cost, permitting lowered market prices while maintaining or increasing rates of return on equity. This would result, along with substantially increased food supplies, in raising the standards of living in metropolitan areas for working-class people.

As with polarized industrial growth in regional centers, the problems in getting started are not trivial. For example, enhancing the opportunities for higher incomes from modernized agriculture by heavy investment in small central places may lead to farm consolidation by local elites.[54] While the net effect will increase agricultural output, inequality in local income distribution may be increased rather than reduced. In this event, the creation of a mass basis for consumption of light consumer goods would not occur. Provision of wider, more stable, and lower-cost services to farmers by townspeople is bound to encounter severe opposition by the twentieth-century *caciques*, whose dominance over the local economy would be threatened. In the few cases where *land* monopoly has been broken up, it has tended to be replaced in the towns by *trade* monopoly— an equally effective means of exploiting the peasant. Since the existence of government control of the countryside often depends upon these townspeople, most governments are understandably reluctant to challenge the system, particularly when they are, in fact, the heart of the system.

At the national level, a strategy based upon fostering the growth of small central places and modernizing agricultural output for domestic consumption would pose severe problems for the balance of payments. Much capital would be required to pay for transport systems, fertilizer plants, agricultural machinery, social overhead, and the dispersion of light, durable consumer-goods industries. There would be little in the way of enhanced production for export. Finally, consumption of fossil fuels would tend to be maximized because of the transport problem in dealing with vast numbers of communities and because of the employment of many smaller machines, which are relatively less energy-efficient than a few large plants. In short, the national implications of this policy for the international balance of payments would be to increase required capital and energy imports while not necessarily generating compensatory increases in exports. The result in terms of national abilities to sustain the urban middle-class consumption of elaborate consumer goods such as household machinery and television sets is obvious, and the level of consumption might have to be sacrificed for some time.[55]

Given the thrust of this century's experience with social class structure in most Latin American countries, the central-place strategy is most unlikely to be adopted in the absence of a profound change in political philosophy and structure. The central-place strategy differs from the ruralist strategy in the assumption that focused investment in the towns will generate a stream of innovative changes in the farming villages. The ruralist strategy instead argues from the premise that reorganization of tenure and production relationships in the *villages* will lead to the creation of the necessary support activities in the towns.[56] It is obvious that both approaches are closely interrelated in time and space. However, the central-place strategy is somewhat more conservative in outlook since it does not necessarily entail serious restructuring of land-tenure arrangements. But note the caution mentioned above concerning potential land consolidation by local elites given new market opportunities, because radical change can go as easily in a conservative direction as in a liberal one.

EXPORT-BASED REGIONAL DEVELOPMENT POLICIES

A good deal of attention since World War II has been given to the matter of trade between the developed and less-developed nations. The GATT (General Agreement on Trade and Tariffs) and more recently UNCTAD (United Nations Conference on Trade and Development) have attacked the set of associated problems from an international perspective. Little attention, though, has been given the intranational, spatial implications for the Third World countries. We will here explore a few implications on a preliminary basis.

Manufactured goods which enjoy a comparative advantage in world trade for Latin American economies are those which encompass a large proportion of labor. These include rather sophisticated goods for which highly simplified assembly operations can be devised. A leading example is the assembly of semiconductor components for electrical equipment and consumer goods such as television sets, radio receivers and transmitters, and remote-sensing devices. Latin American manufacturing establishments that produce these goods usually locate in areas which have easily assembled, literate labor, transportation connections with international markets, and excellent international communications. The assembling of such goods is but one step in a complex international manufacturing process. This combination of locational attributes is found mainly in large port metropolises in Latin America, with the notable exceptions of Mexican highland cities and such inland Brazilian metropolises as São Paulo and Belo Horizonte. But as these goods tend to be high-value, low-bulk commodities, air transport and easy handling reduce the dependence on ports and ocean shipping. Furthermore, export of early import substitutes such as textiles, clothing, footwear and hardware may result as a low-cost use of excess capacity. Indeed, that is the *raison d'être* for the strategy in the first instance and even more will emphasize employment growth in the large industrial cities. In summary, it can be predicted with some confidence that the spatial results of pursuing a national strategy of promotion of industrial exports will be further increases in the growth of central cities in Latin America.

A possible exception to this generalization has already been alluded to. Various plans of international trading within Latin America may produce substantially different patterns of traffic flows and of product mixes. This locational effect already may be seen on some portions of the border between Venezuela and Colombia, in the increased importance of the north Chilean port of Arica, and in the growth of San Pedro Sula in Honduras. This effect will probably remain relatively minor in scope unless and until common-market planners decide deliberately to foster massive growth by infrastructure investments at transport junctions between member states.

AN ASSESSMENT OF SPATIAL DEVELOPMENT POLICIES

Choosing a spatial strategy for development depends in very large measure upon the national choice among alternatives for development, which in turn is conditioned by history and patterned by political forces. Regional analysis and planning contribute to understanding the spatial implications of those national policies.

It has been argued that there is a preferred spatial strategy for development given central decisions concerning the content of development and the segments of society to receive the direct benefits of national developmental investment. Current policies lead to the creation and maintenance of very large urban centers oriented fundamentally toward international markets and supported by small regions of highly capitalized agriculture. Both Mexico and Brazil are large enough to support both heavy industrialization and consumer-goods industries. Both countries have gone very far toward the creation of fully integrated industrial states. Both nations are, however, heavily dependent upon international markets to sustain economic growth in the face of inadequate domestic demand. Most of the rest of Latin America is not so fortunate, and domestic crises associated with excess capacity in industrial plant and employment levels are common.

Essentially, three alternative spatial solutions are proposed for moving beyond the narrow urban middle-class basis for further modernization. These are the growth-center strategy of polarized development, the central-place strategy of town development, and the ruralist strategy of agricultural development. A rational process of making these choices depends upon an understanding of historical experience, the effects of broader central policy, and the opportunities for future social change presented by each alternative.

One aspect of this entire discussion is probably central: All spatial strategies for development have the common objective of creating a hierarchy of centers which would mobilize the human and natural resources of an entire nation. They differ mostly in the scale at which initial efforts ought to be focused. In that context, growth-center policies are but one of a range of alternative solutions to problems of modernizing and integrating national economic space.

POPULATION POLICIES AND REGIONAL DEVELOPMENT

The literature on populaton in Latin America concentrates on the urbanization process and its rapidity due in part to high fertility rates and massive migration. Poverty in the cities is endemic and a disturbing political factor. Most Latin American governments have turned to military forms of rule, partly in response to the instability in the large cities as well as partly in conformance with a long tradition of hierarchic and authoritarian modes of organization. This suggests the possibility that military juntas, in their search for social order, may decide to decentralize growth even at the risk of antagonizing the urban middle class, which has previously been the foundation for the political stability which did exist. Population policies from a spatial perspective will undoubtedly be adopted in effective form only when the basic political decision is taken by either the juntas or their successors in office. Until then, population researchers can only elaborate upon the benefits and the costs of adoption of one or another degree of decentralization of both economic growth and population movement.

Notes

1. *United Nations Demographic Yearbook, 1976*, 26th issue (New York: Department of Economic and Social Affairs, Statistical Office, 1975), Table

6:"Urban and Total Population by Sex"; and also drawing upon 1970–1971 data from the International Bank for Reconstruction and Development *World Bank Operations: Sectoral Programs and Policies* (Baltimore: Johns Hopkins University Press 1972) for data concerning Argentina, the Dominican Republic, Haiti, and Trinidad and Tobago. The percent of the population which is regarded as "urban" in the early 1970s can be classified as follows:

Percent Living in Urban Areas	*Number of Countries*
Above 70	3
60 to 69	4
50 to 59	3
40 to 49	4
30 to 39	6
20 to 29	0
10 to 19	1
0 to 9	0
	21

Thus, ten out of twenty-one countries in Latin America have more than 50 percent of their people living in urban areas. Two of the four countries in the 40 percent to 50 percent range had more than 48 percent urbanized by 1974 and are probably in the more-than-50 percent category by now. Since most of the largest Latin American countries are more urbanized than the smaller countries, the number of people living in countries which are more than 50 percent urbanized is today in excess of 260 million out of a total Latin American population of about 310 million. The percent, therefore, of Latin Americans living in countries more than half urbanized is about 84 percent. Hence, a reasonable estimate is that more than half of all Latin Americans live in urbanized areas (given that the largest nations are. considerably more than 50 percent urbanized, i.e., Argentina—71 percent urban; Brazil—59 percent urban; Colombia—64 percent urban; and Mexico—62 percent urban).

For a recent review of urban prospects in Latin America during the last quarter of this century and the relationship of government policies to the urbanization process, see Frederick Turner, "The Rush to the Cities in Latin America: Government Actions Have More Effect than is Generally Recognized," *Science* 192, no. 4243 (June 4, 1976): 955–62.

2. For a good review of the issues involved in the "urban phase" of Latin American development, see John Miller and Ralph Gakenheimer, *Latin American Urban Policies and the Social Sciences* (Beverly Hills and London: Sage, 1971). Use of the term "hyperurbanization" is found in John Friedmann, *Urbanization, Planning and National Development* (Beverly Hills and London: Sage, 1973); especially see chapter 5, "Hyperurbanization and National Development in Chile," pp. 91–114. However, the

concept is widespread in the literature. For example, see the five-volume (to date) series *Latin American Urban Research*, published by Sage Publications. The most recent issue (Vol. 5) is edited by Wayne Cornelius and Felicity Trueblood and is devoted to "Urbanization and Inequality, The Political Economy of Urban and Rural Development in Latin America."

3. See, for example, B. J. L. Berry, "Comparative Urbanization Strategies," in *Issues in the Management of Urban Systems*, H. Swain and R. D. MacKinnon, eds. (*Papers and Proceedings* from an International Institute for Applied Systems Analysis [IIASA] Conference on National Settlement Systems and Strategies, Schloss Laxemburg, Austria, December 1974), pp. 66–79. This is CP-75-4 of a set of very interesting papers that resulted from the interaction of Communist and Western regional and urban planners under the aegis of IIASA.

4. The most famous study of the location of the Mexican steel industry in Monterrey is R. A. Kennelly, "The Location of the Mexican Steel Industry," *Revista Geográfica*, 15, no. 41 (1954): 109–129; 16, no. 42 (1955): 199–213; 17, no. 43 (1955): 60–77.

5. The classic but now dated study of planning for the petrochemical complex of Puerto Rico is Joseph Airov, *The Location of the Synthetic Fiber Industry: A Study in Regional Analysis* (New York: John Wiley, 1959). More recent evaluations of large chemical complexes installed in Latin America are United Nations Economic Commission for Latin America (ECLA), *The Process of Industrial Development In Latin America,* (New York, 1966), and the UNIDO Monograph #8, idem.

6. John Friedmann, *Regional Development Policy: A Case Study of Venezuela* (Cambridge, Mass.: MIT Press, 1966).

7. For a review of locational requirements of industry in Latin America, see ECLA, *The Process of Industrial Development in Latin America.*

8. The whole question of industrializing by import substitution and then integrating backward toward intermediate goods has been dealt with almost exhaustively by Albert O. Hirshman. For example, see his books, *The Strategy for Economic Development* (New Haven, Conn.: Yale University Press, 1958) and *Journeys toward Progress: Studies of Economic Decision-Making in Latin America* (New York: Twentieth Century Fund, 1963). Benjamin Higgins' *Economic Development, Principles, Problems and Policies*, rev. ed. (New York: W. W. Norton, 1968) is the standard reference work for various theories of economic development. Albert Waterston's *Development Planning: Lessons of Experience* (Baltimore: Johns Hopkins University Press, 1965) has become the standard reference for planning procedures, evaluation methods for projects, and statements of policy criteria.

9. John Friedmann has very accurately portrayed the ultimate results obtained by implementation of the strategy of import substitution coupled with backward linkages in his book *Urbanization, Planning, and National Development*. Especially see chapter 5 (pp. 91–114), entitled "Hyperurbanization and National Development in Chile."

10. For an elaborate discussion of clashes and coalitions between economic

sectors for control over national economic policies toward development, see Markos Mamalakis, "The Theory of Sectoral Clashes," *Latin American Research Review* 4, no. 3 (1969): 9–46.

11. The work most familiar to English-speaking Latin Americanists along these lines is André Gunder Frank, *Capitalism and Underdevelopment in Latin America: Historical Studies of Chile and Brazil* (New York and London: Monthly Review Press, 1967).

12. Archibald Ritter, *The Economic Development of Revolutionary Cuba: Strategy and Performance*, Praeger Special Studies of International Economics and Development (New York: Praeger, 1974).

13. For a review of recent urbanization trends, policies, and problems in Costa Rica, see Leonardo Silva Kind and Eduardo Jenkins Robles, "Desarrollo Urbano en Costa Rica," which is chapter 4 (pp. 55–76) in *Public Policy and Urbanization in the Dominican Republic and Costa Rica*, Gustavo Antonini, ed. (Gainesville: Center for Latin American Studies, University of Florida Press, 1972).

14. "Down Mexico Way," *Monthly Review* The Bank of Nova Scotia, Toronto (May 1976).

15. Friedmann, *Urbanization, Planning, and National Development*, especially chapter 12 (pp. 235–54), "The Implementation of Regional Development Policies: Lessons of Experience."

16. Antoni Kuklinski edited an excellent review of thoughtful articles concerning *Growth Poles and Growth Centers in Regional Planning* (The Hague and Paris: Mouton, 1972). It is volume 9 of a series of publications by the United Nations Research Institute for Social Development (UNRISD). The first chapter, "Development Poles and Development Centers in National and Regional Development: Elements of a Theoretical Framework," by Tormod Hermanson (pp. 1–68), is probably the best single review of the subject to date. Kuklinski has made a number of perceptive comments on the role of regional and town planning in national development in "Regional Development, Regional Policies and Regional Planning," *Regional Studies* 4:269–78, and "Local Governments in Regional and National Perspectives," which is an article in Antoni Kuklinski, ed. *Regional Disaggregation of National Policies and Plans,* (The Hague and Paris: Mouton). UNRISD Series, Regional Planning, No. 8, 1971).

17. Niles Hansen, *French Regional Planning* (Bloomington: Indiana University Press, 1968), and *Rural Poverty and the Urban Crisis: A Strategy for Regional Development* (Bloomington: Indiana University Press, 1970).

18. E. A. J. Johnson has argued persuasively for a policy of deliberate creation of a multitude of small central places based on commercial and service activities, in his book *The Organization of Space in Developing Countries* (Cambridge, Mass.: Harvard University Press, 1970). Especially see chapters 6 and 7 (pp. 178–241), "The Critical Role of Market Towns in Modernizing the Landscapes of Underdeveloped Countries" and "Spatial Reconstruction: Some Policy Aspects," respectively.

19. Jerzy Regulski, "Development Poles Theory and Its Application in Poland," in *Growth Poles and Growth Centers,* Antoni Kuklinski, ed. chapter 9, pp.

207–19. This was published in 1972. For later comments concerning the topic of a national settlement strategy within the context of socialist planning in Poland, see Piotr Korcelli, "Aspects of Polish National Urban Policy," IIASA CP–75–3 (1975), in *National Settlement Strategies East and West*, Harry Swain, ed. (Schloss Laxemburg, Austria). This is a collection of papers presented at an IIASA conference concerning national settlement systems and strategies. In the same volume are articles concerning socialist thinking on settlement strategies in the USSR, the German Democratic Republic, Hungary, and Canada.

20. It is hard to decipher the nature of regional planning apparatus in the People's Republic of China. However, Western scholars seem to be agreed that economic planning is highly decentralized with regard to urban and regional development policies. For example, see K. Buchanan, *The Transformation of the Chinese Earth* (London: G. Bell, 1970); Kuo-Chiin Chao, *Agrarian Policies of Mainland China; A Documentary Study (1949–1957)*, Vols. 1 and 2 (Cambridge, Mass.: Harvard University Press, 1957); and several studies by the Joint Economic Committee of the United States Congress, such as *An Economic Profile of Mainland China* (1968), *The People's Republic of China: An Economic Assessment (1972)* and *Economic Development in Mainland China* (1975).

21. This term appears very early in François Perroux's original conceptualization of growth poles. See "Note sur la notion des poles de croissance," *Economie Appliqué* 1 and 2 (1955).

22. For a review of the meaning of this term and other related concepts as of the late 1960s, see David F. Darwent, "Growth Poles and Growth Centers in Regional Planning—A Review," *Environment and Planning* 1, no. 1 (1969): 5–32. In general, the growth pole is a concept of propulsive industries which are defined in nonspatial terms. Growth centers are places (generally cities) where growth poles locate. Unfortunately, growth centers are often identified as any city which is growing rapidly and where the writer supposes that rapid growth will continue into the future. As such, the term means very little.

23. Friedmann and his associates have been giving the political and especially the information-diffusion aspects of the general theory of polarized development more and more emphasis over the past few years. An excellent example of the key role of diffusion analysis in the theory is found in Walther Stohr, "New Towns and Growth Centers in National Urban Systems—Some Theoretical Spatial-Economic Considerations," IIASA CP-75-4, pp. 155–79. See Swain and MacKinnon (eds.), note 3 for full cite. The problem lies in the meaning of the term "innovative" which, if it implies any change in economic organization, technology, and marketing systems or product, says very little by encompassing all of economic development.

24. While E. A. J. Johnson has made the most determined case for the use of central-place theory (*The Organization of Space in Developing Countries*), see also Lloyd Rodwin, *Nations and Cities: A Comparison of Strategies for Urban Growth* (Boston: Houghton Mifflin, 1970). Koichi Mera, "A Multiple

Layer Theory of National Urban Systems," IIASA CP-75-4, in *Issues in the Management of Urban Systems*, pp. 134–54, presents an attempt to deal with the interrelationships between existing spatial theories in an integrated fashion and to apply a sectorally defined model to the Japanese case. While the results are rather simplistic, the notion is intriguing, especially in light of Markos Mamalakis' theory of sectoral clashes and coalitions. If Mamalakis is correct in ascribing most of the content of political decision-making in Latin American governments to clashes and coalitions of economic sectors, and if Mera is correct in concluding that government is the key city-building sector (followed by industry), then it follows that spatial strategies for development of urban places may be deduced from national policies directed at economic sectors. This, of course, is the major thesis of this chapter.

25. The sheer volume of literature on urbanization in Latin America is enormous. A few of the more readily available general reviews of the subject are Philip Hauser and Leo F. Schnore, eds., *The Study of Urbanization* (New York: John Wiley & Sons, 1965); Gerald Brese, *Urbanization in Newly Developing Countries* (Englewood Cliffs, N.J.: Prentice-Hall, 1966); Lowdon Wingo, Jr., "Recent Patterns of Urbanization Among Latin American Countries," *Urban Affairs Quarterly* 2 (March, 1967): 81–109; John Miller and Ralph Gakenheimer, eds., *Latin American Urban Policies and the Social Sciences* (Beverly Hills and London: Sage, 1971); and an annual volume of solicited papers edited by Francine Rabinowitz and Felicity Trueblood called *Latin American Urban Research*, starting with volume 1 in 1971 and going through volume 5 in 1975 (last available issue) and published by Sage Publications. A couple of examples of planning-oriented literature concerning urbanization in Latin America are Lloyd Rodwin et al., *Planning Urban Growth and Regional Development: The Experience of the Guayana Program in Venezuela* (Cambridge, Mass.: MIT Press, 1969) and Lowdon Wingo, Jr., "Latin American Urbanization: Plan or Process?" in *Shaping an Urban Future*, B. J. Frieden and W. W. Nash, eds. (Cambridge, Mass.: Harvard University Press, 1969).

26. See Richard Morse, "Trends and Issues in Latin American Urban Research, 1965–1970," Part I in *Latin American Research Review* 6, no. 1 (Spring 1971): 3–52, and Part II in *Latin American Research Review* 6, no. 2 (Summer 1971): 19–75. On page 17 Part I, Morse concludes his summary of the Iberian legacy in this way:

In the latter tradition (north European) urban life becomes identified with social change, economic opportunity, personal freedoms, and political radicalism—and subsequently with anomie and social breakdown. Such phenomena are by no means alien to Spanish American cities. But the patrimonial traditions of governance and society within which they developed condition the ways in which innovation is produced or accommodated in the urban setting. Spanish American social organization, attitudes toward authority, social mobility patterns, entrepreneurship and achievement motivation, and urban-rural "dependency" relationships are stamped by the traditions which pressures of commercialism and industrialism can rework but not efface. It is precisely this cross-hatch of cultural commitment and imperatives for change that deserves central focus in urban research in contemporary Latin America.

In terms of this chapter's thesis, these "patrimonial traditions of governance and society" lead to a tendency to centralize all economic decision-making and therefore all decision-makers within the confines of a very few urban centers. In turn, given the tendency of people to perceive opportunities as being greater and risks as being less nearer to home (i.e., the same central cities), there is a pronounced tendency to concentrate new investment around the existing urban centers and to focus the purpose of those investments upon the urban middle class. Of course, this results in the primacy patterns for which Latin America is justly so famous.

27. See Harry Bernstein, *Modern and Contemporary Latin America* (Chicago: J. B. Lippincott, 1952) for an excellent review and evaluation of nineteenth-century political regionalism in Mexico, Argentina, Brazil, Chile, and Colombia.

28. The Bernstein book is also very good for this period. ECLA's *The Process of Industrial Development in Latin America* picks up the story of Latin American industrialization in the Depression of the 1930s and carries it through the period of import substitution to the early 1960s.

29. See Diaz Alejandro, *Essays on Argentine Economic History* (New Haven, Conn.: Yale University Press, 1970).

30. The Guayana Project has long been a focus of interest for North American students of regional development. For example, see Hirshman's 1963 study *Journeys toward Progress*, Friedmann's 1966 study *Regional Development Policy*, and Lloyd Rodwin's 1970 study *Nations and Cities*.

31. Although flawed by excessive polemical zeal in putting forth a classic Marxian interpretation of Latin American development, André Gunder Frank's analysis of the colonial and nineteenth-century economic history of Chile and Brazil makes very much the same point (see *Capitalism and Underdevelopment in Latin America*).

32. For a review of the major features of these analyses, see Waterston, *Development Planning*.

33. There are innumerable discussions of the marginally employed urban populations in Latin American primate cities during the 1970s in *Finance and Development*, which is a quarterly publication of the International Monetary Fund and the World Bank. To cite only one recent example, see Callisto Eneas Modavo, "Uncontrolled Settlements," 13, no. 1 (March 1976): 16–19.

34. See footnote 8.

35. Markos Mamalakis, "The Theory of Sectoral Clashes and Coalitions Revised," *Latin American Research Review* 6, no. 3 (1971): 89–126. Perhaps a single sentence on page 108 can give the flavor of what Mamalakis has argued: "The biggest obstacle to Latin American development has been the continuity of its defective allocation process, which persistently di-

rected resource surpluses to the support of cities, services and consumption, and considered such surpluses as divine gifts."

36. The evidence for the spatial structure of innovation diffusion in Latin America is very thin. Stohr argues ("New Towns and Growth Centers") that the diffusion process is dominated by the effect of distance from the major metropolitan center in less developed countries and by hierarchical diffusion patterns (i.e., from top to bottom) in more developed nations. The only empirically based study of the relationship of diffusion processes to urban-regional development of which I am aware in the Latin American context is Paul O. Pederson, *Urban-Regional Development in South America: A Process of Diffusion and Integration* (The Hague: Mouton, 1975). Since the spatial structure of concentrated innovations generation and subsequent polarized diffusion is a theory yet to be firmly established at the empirical level, making innovation diffusion the centerpiece for a general theory of urbanization in developing nations would appear a priori to be tendentious. Additionally, it also seems to be unnecessary in accounting for the observed facts of urbanization in Latin America.

37. The evidence for the market orientation of consumer-goods industries, on the other hand, is massive. For example, see Allen R. Pred, *The Spatial Dynamics of U.S. Urban-Industrial Growth, 1800–1914* (Cambridge, Mass.: MIT Press, 1966), and David M. Smith, *Industrial Location* (New York: John Wiley & Sons, 1971).

38. For a brief but very well-written evaluation of regional growth patterns in Brazil of the late 1960s, see Pedro Geiger and Fany Davidovitch, "Urban Growth as a Factor of Regional Balance-Imbalance," in *Proceedings of the Commission on Regional Aspects of Development of the International Geographical Union*, Vol. I: *Methodology and Case Studies*, Richard Thoman, ed. (1974), pp. 153, 171. The volume contains a number of references to urbanization in Brazil from the viewpoint of growth-center theory.

39. See footnote 9.

40. See Stohr's recent elaboration of this point (footnotes 23 & 36).

41. Paul N. Rosenstein-Rodan, "Notes on the Theory of the 'Big Push' " (Cambridge, Mass.: Center for International Studies, MIT, 1957). Reprinted in more accessible form in *Economic Development in Latin America*, I.E.A. (New York: Macmillan, 1963).

42. See footnotes 11 and 31.

43. Much of this program is implied in Frank's "Capitalism and the Myth of Feudalism in Brazilian Agriculture," which is chapter 4 of *Capitalism and Underdevelopment in Latin America*. For a more recent analysis leading to much the same conclusions, see Ernest Feder, *The Rape of the Peasantry: Latin America's Landholding System* (Garden City, N.Y.: Anchor Books, 1971). A broad-ranging survey of the dependency thesis applied to Latin America is James D. Crockroft, André Gunder Frank and Dale L. Johnson, *Dependence and Underdevelopment: Latin America's Political Economy* (Garden City, N.Y.: Anchor Books, 1972). Non-Marxian views of agrarian problems in Latin America are surveyed in Rodolfo Stavenhagen, ed.,

Agrarian Problems and Peasant Movements in Latin America (Garden City, N.Y.: Anchor Books, 1970).

44. L. B. Fletcher and W. C. Merrill, *Latin American Agricultural Development and Policies*, International Studies in Economics, Monograph No. 8 (Iowa State University, September 1968).

45. Possibly the best single summary of agricultural development studies of the 1950–1969 period is Clifton Wharton, Jr., ed., *Subsistence Agriculture and Economic Development* (Chicago: Aldine, 1969). Possibly the most succinct statement of the best Western advice on agricultural development from a Western perspective was phrased in the form of a "recipe" by the famous agricultural economist Earl O. Heady in "Processes and Priorities in Agricultural Development," which is chapter 4 of *Economic Development of Tropical Agriculture*, W. W. McPherson, ed. (Gainesville: University of Florida Press, 1968), p. 63: "Lower prices and increased availability of resources, add certainty and quantity to produce prices, blend with knowledge and a firm or tenure structure which relates input productivities appropriately with resource/product price ratios." Of course, the recipe, like all recipes, does not tell how to "blend" and to "relate." However, I believe the statement covers all of the essential points to be made.

46. Feder (footnote 43) notes this problem on pp. 275–92. The fact is that a serious program of rural development requires both political changes in land-tenure conditions and a *significant* transferral of capital investment from urban to rural settings. It is clear that changing the emphasis in the location of capital investment can only be accomplished by major changes in the sectoral pattern of economic planning, and it is also clear that this sectoral change involves major considerations in the political economy. Once again, we return to basic decisions which are essentially nonspatial and are the key to spatial strategies for development in Latin America.

47. Friedmann has constantly revised and expanded his definitions of the "periphery" which, in his earlier versions of growth-center theory, were the negative complement of the "core." A number of authors have critically reviewed the lack of adequate classification of areas within the core–periphery paradigm. For example, see Howard Gauthier's perceptive criticism, "Economic Growth and Growth Poles: A Search for Geographic Theory?" in *Proceedings of the Commission on Regional Aspects of Development of the International Geographic Union*, Vol. II: *Spatial Aspects of the Development Process*, F. Helleiner and W. Stohr, eds. (1974), pp. 19–31. The industrial base of growth poles is probably the only common element in the far-ranging discussions and debates which have enveloped the subject of spatial strategies for development over the past seven years.

48. While it is difficult to cite specific sources for this brief compendium, the criteria listed in the text repeatedly appear in the references already cited and also in Niles M. Hansen, *Growth Centers in Regional Economic Development* (New York: The Free Press, 1972).

49. Many of these positive incentives are discussed by Friedmann in *Urbanization, Planning, and National Development* in chapter 12, section III, pp. 243–48, "Concerning the Use of Instruments for Regional Development."

50. The French have made strenuous efforts over the past ten to fifteen years to decentralize economic growth and population concentration in the Paris region. Probably the best single review of French regional economic thought by the late 1960s is Niles M. Hansen, *French Regional Planning* (Bloomington: Indiana University Press, 1968). An elaborate attempt to regionalize national economic planning is the REGINA model prepared for the Seventh Development Plan of France, to start in 1975 under the direction of Raymond Courbis. The model is a medium-term econometric forecasting tool with some 7,000 equations. A report of the structure of the model can be found in *Environment and Planning*, 7, no. 7 (1975).

51. For a succinct review of Say's Law, see J. Henderson and R. Quandt, *Microeconomic Theory: A Mathematical Approach*, 2nd ed. (New York: McGraw-Hill, 1971), pp. 177–78. The reason for equating the arguments of growth-center strategies with this nineteenth-century classical theory is that most growth-center theorists blithely tend to ignore the role of the spatial distribution and quantity of demand for the industrial products of new industrial centers in accounting for their locations. This is not true of Perroux's original statement defining propulsive industries (the definition of the "growth pole" itself) in part as those industries which enjoyed rapidly expanding demand for their products owing to a high income elasticity of demand. The implicit argument of recent statements by growth-center advocates seems to involve the assumption that somehow innovative changes in economic organization and technology will *generate* growth. This must involve implicitly some parallel assumption that this growth in production will be accompanied by concomitant growth in demand—hence Say's Law. The role of income distribution and hence the monetized demand for industrial production is ignored.

52. See footnote 18.

53. See Johnson, *The Organization of Space in Developing Countries*, especially chapter 3, pp. 72–116, "Market Systems and Spatial Design."

54. See Johnson, chapter 11, "Some Guidelines for Spatial Policy."

55. A recent example of this is the Swedish experiences with induced agricultural development focused on market towns in Ethiopia; John M. Cohen, "Rural Change in Ethiopia: The Chilalo Agricultural Development Unit," *Economic Development and Cultural Change* 22, no. 4 (July 1974): 580–614.

56. President Julius Nyerere's Tanzanian experiment in decentralized, rurally oriented socialist development has attracted worldwide attention because of its unique features. A few basic references on Nyerere's policies are Julius K. Nyerere, *Ujamaa—Essays on Socialism* (Dar es Salaam: Oxford University Press, 1968); Lionel Cliffe and John S. Small, eds., *Socialism in Tanzania* (Dar es Salaam: East Africa Publishing House, 1972); William L. Luttrell, "Location Planning and Regional Development in Tanzania," in *Towards Socialist Planning*, J. F. Rweyemamu, et al, eds. (Dar es Salaam: Tanzania Publishing House, 1972); and Gerritt Huzier, "The Ujamaa Village Program in Tanzania: New Forms of Rural Development," *Studies in Comparative International Development* 8, no. 2 (1973): 183–207.

J. Barry Riddell

African Migration and Regional Disparities

Human mobility is a response to variations in the environmental and ecological conditions within which people live. As the physical landscape evolves through time, social and political circumstances change, economic conditions fluctuate, and the individual progresses through the natural life cycle, people move from place to place. Migration is the basic response to altering situations. Within West Africa, however, differences in these influencing factors, though important in some scales of analysis, are rather minor when considered within the same context as the impact of European colonialism and the attainment of national independence. Because of the fundamental importance of these two factors, a description of the causes and characteristics of migration in West Africa is much more meaningful when placed in a historical context.

Migration in West Africa: A Historical Perspective

HUMAN MOBILITY IN TRADITIONAL SOCIETY

It would be false to suggest that human mobility in West Africa was either nonexistent or strictly limited prior to the period of European imperial expansion. No firm documentation exists in the form of written records or census tabulations, but sufficient oral and archaeological evidence indicates that precolonial movement was widespread and common. Essentially, these population movements were of two types, one associated with fluctuations in political suzerainty and the other with economic circumstances. The former was coupled with the gradually expanding areal expression of empires. Examples abound and include Songhai, Ghana, and Mali. The latter, in contrast, was much more peaceful in nature and involved the movement of peasants—farmers and pastoralists—in search of better lands for their crops and animals. Usually such movements were associated with times and places where political structures were weak and frontiers ill defined.

Such historical movements led to the gradual transformation of significantly large areas, in that whole cultures and societies diffused spatially,
and institutions and artifacts were transported. In a similar fashion,
agricultural systems could be dramatically altered and political frameworks changed. It is likely that such movements were of sufficient magnitude to alter the distributions of population and population density.

Such movements were much more difficult than are similar population
migrations today, especially at the individual or family level. There were
real and effective restraints to movement. The hundreds of language
groups found throughout West Africa meant that a great deal of prepara-
tion or adjustment had to accompany movement. Nor did an individual
leaving his own ethnic group often gain higher social status. In fact, he
was more likely to lose and to become a stranger in an alien world.
Improved means of transportation were largely nonexistent; roads were
few, and throughout the southern part of the area, animals were unavail-
able because of trypanosomiasis. When roads did exist, they were seldom
free of obstruction and extortion. Finally, the frictional effects of distance,
especially in terms of time and cost, were extremely high, and information
on nonlocal opportunities was seldom available. Just as today, there were
certain groups within the population who were most able and willing to
move about—or who perhaps did so because of economic necessity. Also,
there were traders and merchants who moved within certain facilitating
niches and arrangements, best exemplified by the *sabron garis* and the
landlords found in widely dispersed parts of the countryside.

THE IMPACT OF THE COLONIAL PERIOD

The influences of European adventurers and traders began to be felt in
parts of West Africa early in the sixteenth century. The most dramatic
effects of the colonial period with respect to migration coincided with the
imposition of direct colonial rule at the turn of the twentieth century.
Britain and France especially, but also to a lesser extent Germany,
Portugal, and Spain, drew lines upon the map of West Africa representing
the bounds of their new colonial territories. Nomenclature varied, as did
the form of colonial rule, but certain characteristics which affected mobility were common throughout the area.

European law and order were imposed primarily as essential for the
efficient operation of the colonial commercial enterprises. But peace and
security also meant that people could move without fear of physical
maltreatment. Also, the legal systems of the colonial powers, which were
liberal regarding mobility, were superimposed upon the many local codes
which discouraged travel and migration.

New foci were created as wage employment developed rapidly. Essentially, the jobs for wages were in the several mining enterprises, in the commercial agricultural areas, and in the evolving urban system imposed by the hierarchical colonial structures and the nascent externally oriented trading system. In effect, a new set of niches became available; deviants, misfits, and adventurers from traditional rural society had a place to go— "the city that made men free." Money could be earned, if only at extremely low rates of pay.

The Europeans also revolutionized transportation. New roads were built and railways constructed, and gradually wheeled and then motorized vehicles came to ply the roads. Trypanosomiasis was never eliminated, but its effect on beasts of burden was in large part overcome.

Several phenomena encouraged movement, and the colonial powers intentionally stimulated movement. In West Africa, the British imposed taxes, and those not involved in commercial agriculture had to move from their traditional home areas to earn the tax money in the new mines, cities, or commercial farms. Other needs for money arose as European products became available in the trading centers. The French, in contrast, employed forced labor throughout most of the colonial period, not only for military and public works, but also to provide for the labor needs of private entrepreneurs. Instances of the use of labor recruiters, so common in South and Central Africa, were few in West Africa.

During this period, the character of migration changed in certain basic ways. Movement increased in volume, and the distances traversed multiplied. Economically motivated migration expanded in relative importance, and individual as opposed to group mobility took on greater moment. Population distribution was influenced because many areas which were formerly no-man's-lands between rival tribal groups became settled as law and order eliminated intergroup warfare. There were also instances of downward movements of certain small tribal groups from densely settled hill sites to which they had fled prior to the colonial period in partial defense against the slaving activities of neighboring groups.

Movement into the area by a small but significant group of non-Africans was facilitated and encouraged during the colonial period. Never was land alienated to Europeans on a scale similar to that of Kenya and southern Africa, but Syrians and Lebanese moved into parts of West Africa, gradually influencing and controlling part of the trading systems. In French West Africa, a small group of French nationals moved in to establish plantations and commercial enterprises.

During this period, disparities between areas and differences among groups of people grew and began to be commonly perceived. At the same time, facilities for movement and transportation were provided, which had the effect of easing the human movements which resulted. Perhaps the greatest differential was that which came to exist between the new, large urban center and the traditional rural society. In fact, investigators have suggested a "push-pull" framework for the analysis of the migration factors, which can be termed centrifugal when they include forces which push people from the traditional rural settings, and centripetal when they pull potential migrants toward the urban centers. A host of factors may be listed, but economic forces and economic motives are dominant, and increasingly so, in the decision to make a rural–urban movement.

There are several forces within rural society which influence and even force people to move to seek opportunities beyond the bounds of traditional agricultural pursuits. Although average conditions suggest that West Africa is not suffering from an excessive population in terms of the resource base, there are specific areas where the density of population in relation to the carrying capacity of the physical environment is such that population pressure occurs. Through time, the overcropping associated with land hunger leads to soil erosion and a decreasing carrying capacity of the land. A vicious cycle begins once the delicate symbiotic relationship among climate, vegetation, and soil is weakened. Since there are few safeguards against natural hazards, people are forced to leave rural areas because of such events as fire, pest, and drought. If the crops are destroyed or if they fail, there are few means to overcome the hardship imposed—in the extreme form, starvation. During the colonial period, because of significant improvements in health care and because of the elimination of internecine conflict, death rates were markedly reduced, and the resultant population increase led to heightened pressure on the resource base.

Some, especially the young, found traditional authority, ascription, and stratification to be insufferable and wished to move away from the traditional family and village context. In certain areas, the opening of schools, first by Christian missionaries and later by local and national governments, led to the introduction of Western education, which created new aspirations which could not be satisfied within traditional rural, tribal society. At the same time, skills were imparted which have proved to be more suited to urban than rural employment, and the knowledge of available opportunities in the wider world beyond the village was introduced.

Economic necessity often pushed men out of traditional society to work for wages. Taxes had to be paid, building supplies purchased, educational expenses settled; and new goods, such as radios and bicycles, required income which cannot be earned within the traditional rural schema. Often, however, it was not a matter of absolute economic necessity which drove persons to migrate from rural societies. It was the perception of relative deprivation which is more vital—the realization that to remain in rural society means poverty, while a move to the city may provide the chance of economic advancement.

At the same time, the new and growing urban places apparently offered certain advantages and amenities far different from and far superior to those found in rural traditional society. First was the opportunity for earning money wages so necessary for a better life, for the new European goods, and to pay the taxes imposed by the colonial powers. Such opportunities were severely limited in rural areas because the main source of cash income, the production of export crops was severely limited by the cost of overcoming the distance to the trading port and by yet another set of taxes, those on exports.

There were educational advantages to the town, also. Schooling was more readily available, and the likelihood that one's children would attain the advantages of schooling was increased by urban residence. This was even more true of secondary than of primary education. In addition, the town's bright lights, both literal and figurative, attracted many. Electrical lights and nighttime activity are atypical of rural areas, and the city appears gay and exciting. The bars, brothels, cinemas, dance halls, and shops are radically different from traditional society. For some, the town, with its lack of traditional restrictions, was thought to be a place of unlimited opportunity, and a young man had the chance of rapid social and economic advancement.

Meanwhile, town–village linkages were augmented in a number of ways. Perhaps most obvious was the fact that places were brought closer together, if not in miles, then certainly in terms of cost and effort, by the new railways and roads. The lorries and mammy wagons became ubiquitous, and cheap transport was offered and even promoted.

Most significant, however, was the operation of the two processes of "chain" and "stepwise" migration. Chain migration implies that once some members—even one—of the village or family have moved to an urban destination, they send back information to those remaining behind, usually stressing the glowing opportunities at the destination. They also provide a place in the strange new urban environment to which intending migrants can go upon arrival; there, friends and relatives speak the same language, the new migrant can be housed and fed, and leads are often provided to employment opportunities. Thus the strange and distant city is made far less formidable, and many of the barriers to migration, especially those of information, language, and family relationships are removed. Migration is facilitated, and certain families and many areas thus become "migration prone."

As well as the large urban destinations, there are many small cities and towns dotted across the rural landscape which act as stepping-stones in the migration process. Although the economic opportunities of these centers are fewer and their bright lights are duller than those of large cities, to many potential rural migrants, such centers are viable alternatives in relatively close proximity; the psychological barriers associated with language, diet, and cultural differences are less extreme than with the strange and distant city. Thus, not only is the economic friction of distance reduced in that these intermediate centers are closer, but the psychological interval is lessened. In such a quasi-urban setting, the migrant and his children are exposed to urban jobs, attitudes, and educational opportunities; thus, the social distance to the large city is reduced, and the likelihood of movement to the large and distant city is increased, if not for the current generation, then certainly for the next.

THE COMING OF INDEPENDENCE

Although the granting of independence to the countries of West Africa began in 1957 with Ghana, it was delayed in some territories until as late as 1974. However, for the sake of discussion, the main features coincident with independence can be considered jointly, although it must be recalled that there were temporal differences. Although these West African nations gained their political independence and the former French and British governors were replaced by a new set of African presidents and prime ministers, very little changed in an economic sense; the countries of West Africa still remain economic dependencies, though now of an expanded group of industrialized nations and international corporations.

Perhaps the most notable alteration in migration activity has been the great acceleration in migration to urban centers. This phenomenon has been so pronounced and general throughout the area that predictions have been made that the West African nations will replicate the population distribution of the industrialized countries, with at least two-thirds of their population living in urban centers.

There were important changes associated with the end of the colonial period which led directly to this increase in urban in-migration. When the Europeans departed, their administrative jobs began to be filled by African nationals. As these jobs were urban, the urban centers became more attractive, not only because of these specific openings, but also because of those created further down the employment chain. Of special note in this regard is the fact that eight new nation-states, each with its own administrative bureaucracy, emerged from the former French colony of French West Africa. As well, most nations expanded employment opportunities in industry (largely urban-based) in an attempt both to push on to the road to economic development and to overcome the currency problems associated with the vast array of goods which had to be imported. Although difficult to measure, a psychological barrier was removed at independence from between the cities, which were seen as the centers of foreign white colonial control, and the black rural areas. With independence, the city became an integral part of the black nation. To augment these factors, the very nature of migration has been gradually changing; conditions in the city have improved in terms of wages, housing, and welfare, so that the dominant part of the immigrant streams is no longer unaccompanied males coming to the town for a limited period to earn money, but is composed of families making more permanent moves into the city.

The exodus of Europeans from Africa, especially marked in East Africa, has not been important in West Africa, as there were few European settlers. In fact, there are likely more whites in West Africa today than during the colonial period; but the character of the white community has somewhat changed. Today it is largely comprised of temporary residents on pedagogic, technical, or voluntary assignments, rather than of a more permanent class of colonial administrators.

Unfortunately, there has been a great increase in the expulsion of many West Africans from neighboring states, as the frustrations of postindependence economic stagnation have often been vented on foreigners—even other Africans. This has occurred both at the international (e.g., Ghana's 1969 expulsion decree) and the intranational (the events prior to the Biafran secession in Nigeria) levels. At the same time, international borders within West Africa have become greater barriers to movement with the imposition of a series of migration-limiting forces, ranging from duties to outright prohibition.

FUTURE SCENARIOS

Migration and urbanization are complementary processes, acting in a mutual cause-effect system; large urban centers attract migrants, and migration makes urban places grow. It is noted above that there was a rapid increase in urban in-migration in the immediate postcolonial period. It might thus be supposed that the overwhelming majority of Africans would soon become urban dwellers—not to mimic the experience of the industrial countries, but because of economic factors associated with economies of scale, because of the spatial concentration of health and educational facilities, and because of the posssibility of higher individual incomes and standards of living there. However, such a scenario is doubtful. There will be a brake applied to the urbanization process, and there is evidence that this has already begun to occur. The massive levels of unemployment in the large cities of West Africa are the indicator.

The fact is that urbanization of the population requires some economic support base; people must not only be physically housed in urban places, but they must also find employment. However, the nations of West Africa are essentially primary producers on the periphery of the world capitalistic system. As such, their prospects for industrialization are limited, and it is doubtful that the African cities can continue to experience growth simply by taking in each other's washing. In addition, even where limited industrial growth does occur, it tends to be highly capital-intensive, with little capacity for labor absorption. In a sense, then there is a paradox. On the one hand, there is the lack of an urban growth mechanism, while on the other, there are many forces which in the past have led to increasing urbanization—reduction of the frictional effect of distance, the spread of education, and increasing urban minimum wages. Perhaps the future holds a combination of the two—massive urban poverty, with internal forces inducing increasing urbanization of the population and international structures limiting the economic base.

The second speculation relates to the influence which alternative development paths might have on human mobility and the pattern of migration. The nations of West Africa, to greater and lesser degrees, have all followed an essentially Western capitalistic developmental path. The result, in terms of factors related to mobility, has been described above. Tanzania, an East African country, provides an example of a country in Africa which has begun to follow a different developmental path, one that has distinct implications for human mobility. Briefly, since Nyerere's Arusha Declaration of 1967, similarities, not differences, in both the areal and individual senses, have been stressed. So, too, have rural as opposed to urban activities. The national government has undertaken to reduce the urban-rural wage differential, decentralize urban development, limit welfare disparities, and dampen the primal importance of Dar es Salaam by transferring its capital functions inland to the town of Dodoma. China has followed a similar path, and the level of urbanization of the population has ceased to grow over the past decade and perhaps has even decreased. The lesson for West Africa in terms of migration is fairly simple: Migration is part of a much larger system of change, which includes urbanization, education, industrialization, regional disparities, etc. If the process whereby these forces are directed is altered (i.e., developmental path through economic development planning), then mobility will be transformed as well.

OSCILLATING MIGRATION AND ITS EVOLUTION THROUGH
ALTERING CIRCUMSTANCES

When they migrate to urban areas, a large number of migrants do not do so on a permanent basis. Rather, their movement might be termed

migrant
oscolation

oscillation, in that they return to the rural home after spending a period of time in urban wage employment. In fact, it was likely true only a few years ago that the majority of Africans living in towns and cities were only temporarily urbanized. They were urban residents loyal to a rural home and living in a dual system. For several reasons (to be outlined below), such circulation between rural and urban areas has decreased through time in West Africa, though it is still important and has left a legacy of urban–rural remittances, visitations, psychological links, and often long-term circulation.

The migrants traditionally moved into urban places for short periods of time, varying in length from a few weeks to several years. Their roots were in the rural areas, to which they returned to find wives, maintain land rights, build houses, and retire. For some, the urban movement was a short-term venture lasting only a brief period of time; others might have spent a lifetime alternating back and forth between rural, traditional society and the urban situation. Such a pattern of mobility in the past was conditioned by the need to earn cash income to pay taxes or to purchase needed goods, while at the same time by the wish to remain part of traditional society for rational economic and social reasons. It was made necessary by the fact that urban centers were difficult places in which to reconstitute family life. Housing was in short supply; prices were generally high; welfare schemes did not exist for the worker experiencing illness, old age, or unemployment. As well, mortality rates were high in the urban centers during the early part of the colonial period.

Such circular mobility is or has been common throughout much of the remainder of sub-Saharan Africa; it was purposely reduced in the Katanga and Copperbelt areas of Zaire and Zambia because of the economics of the mining firms, and it continues today in South Africa, very ably enforced by rules, regulations, and laws. As well, it was a common form of population mobility in Western Europe at the turn of the nineteenth century.

However, there is evidence in West Africa that such periodic urban-directed mobility is diminishing in relative importance. Migrants on the average are remaining longer in towns, and the urban labor force is stabilizing. Several factors are important in causing this transition. Urban unemployment is mounting, and workers are reluctant to leave jobs for a temporary sojourn to the rural areas, only to return to a difficult labor market. As well, urban wage rates are now significantly higher and can provide a suitable family income despite the inflated urban cost of living; private and public welfare services are being provided in the towns; health care is better than in the rural areas, and educational facilities are much more common. But despite the fact that oscillating migration is on the wane, the rural–urban link remains strong for the majority. It is expressed no longer by short-term circular migration between the rural and urban settings, but by the sending of remittances home, by frequent visitations, and by the building of rural homes for eventual retirement. In fact, there is evidence that in some areas at least, the traditional rural extended family now exists with both urban and rural branches in intimate contact, though often separated by great distance.

Research on West African Migration: An Overview

There has been a great deal of research into African migration. These investigations have employed several explanatory frameworks, models, or modes of explanation, including gravity models, human capital investment theory, push-pull frameworks, and the mover-strayer dichotomy. The wide variation in these separate research efforts is partly a result of the limited availability of data on migration. More important, however, is the fact that the studies are conditioned by the several disciplinary orientations of the workers, who include geographers, demographers, sociologists, economists, regional scientists, anthropologists, and planners—each with a separate respective disciplinary paradigm or overriding point of view. However, among this variegated amalgam, four quite distinct research perspectives can be identified in the literature:

1. The description of the phenomenon of migration, including its areal patterns of intensity as they may vary in time and space.
2. The investigation of the causes of migration, especially those causal forces associated with variations in interregional streams of migrants and those at the individual level which distinguish between the characteristics of the mobile and of the nonmobile sectors of the populaton.
3. Consideration of the consequences of migration activity in both the host areas and each of the economic, social, political, and environmental senses.
4. The evaluation of the planning, policy, and program implications of such findings.

Hundreds of studies of migration, labor force, employment, and economic development either directly or indirectly pertain to West Africa and could be placed within such a classificatory framework. In most cases, the particular study would fall within several of the above-mentioned categories; the four research perspectives are intimately welded together, and most pieces of research or analysis consider several of the perspectives in an interrelated fashion.

However, the four perspectives can and should be related to a common focus, developing a *theory of human mobility in the West African context*. Obviously, such a framework does not exist other than in intuitive pieces in a few people's minds, but certain of its necessary characteristics can be defined. First, the theory must be inductively based; human mobility in West Africa differs in kind and not just degree from that of Western experience, and models and generalizations transferred from Western literature may hamper an understanding of the migration process in West Africa and will certainly introduce biases into its conceptualization. Second, the theory will have a basis in general systems theory, because migration is part of a large, interacting, and interrelated bundle of changes, which the nations of West Africa are experiencing. These changes include urbanization, rural transformation, educational expansion, commercialization of interpersonal relationships, and so on. All of these are mutually part of a complex cause–effect system, and it is naive, if not dishonest, to treat any one aspect of the system as being simply determined by some or all of the others. Finally, the theory and empirical research will be cross-fertilizing, and there will be fruitful feedback links between empirical and theoretical developments.

Then, from this theoretical base, which implies an intimate understanding of the migration process and the migration mechanism, we will be able to move realistically into areas of policy and planning implementation as well as to attempt predictions or projections of future movements and population distributions.

A NOTE ON THE DIFFERENCES IN MIGRATION IN WEST AFRICA AS COMPARED WITH INDUSTRIAL COUNTRIES

Many have considered that the countries of the Third World are following the same path of economic growth as the industrialized countries, the only difference being that they are somewhat further behind. The Rostow model, outlining the so-called stages of economic growth, is perhaps the most evident example, but the idea has permeated much of the writing on economic development.[1] Here it is necessary to indicate that in terms of population mobility, the Third World experience, as represented by that of West Africa, is different from that of the industrialized countries, even when those countries are considered in their historical setting.

Modern migration in the countries of the Western world might be described as representing an equilibrium type of movement. Most variation in interregional migration is accounted for by rather elementary forms of gravity or opportunity models, the few minor deviations from these very general frameworks being associated with relatively slight interregional differences in wages, employment, and climate. However, migrations in West Africa represent a disequilibrium type of movement, involving masses of unskilled workers moving in response to large relative differences in urbanization, wage-employment opportunities, economic growth, and the location of welfare facilities such as schools and hospitals. The opening of new roads, the extension of education, the provision of new job opportunities—all these have a profound and revolutionary impact upon migration behavior. The former may be typified as human mobility within a fixed-space economy; the latter, as the migration response to an evolving-space economy.

In may ways, it is tempting to think of today's migration in West Africa as mirroring the past experience of the West. Certainly the oscillating nature of current mobility in many parts of West Africa was found in Britain and France in the late eighteenth and early nineteenth centuries. However, the migration experience is fundamentally different. The African migrant is not usually a person displaced from the land by enclosure or population pressure; he is a landholder or one with land rights. Because of this, the ties between urban and rural areas have been maintained through visitations and remittances in some or all of the economic, social, cultural, and psychological senses. Rural and urban areas are not being transformed simultaneously in Africa as was true of many areas of Europe; African cities are "exploding cities in unexploding economies." The absorptive capacity of urban industries is also different—the labor-intensive factories of the European past are represented by relatively capital-intensive activities in Africa today. The difference is represented by the massive and growing unemployment of the cities of West Africa. When the nations of Europe were at the same level of urbanization as those of Africa today, their levels of industrial employment were approximately twice as great. As well, a vital factor is the terms of the power of these countries, not only in international markets, but in their own—and here, too, the nations of West Africa are distinctly disadvantaged. Finally there is no such international-migration safety valve open to the excess urban in-migrants of West Africa as North America presented to Western Europe.

A Geographic Model of Migration: A Macroscopic Perspective

Migration is the result of massive changes which have been occurring over at least the last century in West Africa. Such changes reflect the contact between the colonizer and the colonized. This series of alterations can be viewed as taking place on two distinct scales, and any analysis of the effect of such colonial-induced changes upon migration behavior must recognize

*ecolog-
cal
(models)*

such a dichotomy. On the grossest of scales are the macro forces, those whose effects are on the scale of the region or nation-state. Examples include urbanization, the spread of modern transportation technology, and regional differentials in economic growth. At the same time, certain pressures act at the personal level, affecting individuals. Such are the micro forces, and they include factors such as evolving perceptions and mental images, educational experiences, and life-cycle progression. The literature on migration in West Africa and many of the research efforts to investigate this phenomenon have confused these two scales. In fact, this is entirely understandable, as there is a complex interaction between the two; they act simultaneously and mutually affect one another.

M/R   Here, however, only those macro forces which geographers have tradi-tionally labeled areal differentiation will be discussed. That is, one part of the area experiences positive changes, while the other part remains at a constant level or changes in the opposite direction. To mention only one index of such change in West Africa: certain areas received all the educational efforts of the several proselytizing Christian missions, and many of the people residing in these areas found important niches in the civil service; those from areas beyond mission contact did not experience Western education until late in the colonial period, if at all, and thus persons from such areas were disadvantaged in terms of not having acquired certain of the skills seen as necessary to become members of the administrative bureaucracy.[2] The point is that when these changes associ-ated with colonial contact took place, some parts of West Africa reaped the benefits, while others felt the backwash.

Population mobility results from and reflects such differentiation. By moving, people are responding to differences in employment opportuni-ties, wages, and welfare facilities (health, education, etc.) in various locations. In a historical context in West Africa, the massive movements of people from rural interior settings to the cities and towns and to the near-coastal commercial-agriculture areas reflect this human response. Such differentials account for the greatest part of the variation in interre-gional migration streams, in diversity in rates of out-migration from areas, and in rates of in-migration. The micro forces, very briefly discussed above, account for the incidence of migration—that is, they are related to questions concerned with who moves and when.

Not long ago, it was popular for geographers to talk about "center-periphery models of economic development" and the "diffusion of mod-ernization." Under these frameworks, the great areal differences which accompanied colonialism were viewed as a reflection of the early stages of the process of economic development. The benefits of the core areas, with their higher levels of education, income, health care, and so forth, were seen as gradually spreading outward to the rest of the country. Today, some are beginning to feel that such a proposition is mistaken and that the advantages of the core area have not and will not spread to the periphery, given the existing political and economic frameworks.[3] In the editorial introduction to a recent book, *Modern Migrations in West Africa,* Samir Amin places population migration in West Africa into the framework of the dependency-underdevelopment model. The areal differentiation of West Africa is simply the result of changes occurring at the dependent periphery of the international capitalistic system. Population is moving as a response to this externally conditioned situation.[4] In fact, such a framework is not in conflict with the traditional economist's model of migration as human capital investment, as modified by Michael Todaro to fit the Third World context.[5] In this model, interregional migration is essentially viewed as a function of the difference in the present value of income streams in the origin (rural) and destination (urban) areas, discounted by the likelihood of urban unemployment and offset by factors relating to the frictional effects of distance.

An Example of Migration to African Cities[6]

Figures 1 and 2 represent cartographic portrayals of a number of sets of information collected by the 1963 population census of Sierra Leone.[7] Here, some remarks will be made on a macroscopic investigation of migration to Freetown, the capital city of Sierra Leone and the largest urban place in this set of destinations. Subsequently, some comparative remarks will be made to relate the migration experience of that city to those of the other nine urban centers (each having somewhat distinct locational, administrative, economic, and social characteristics).

The city of Freetown is in one important sense similar to the large capitals of the nations of West Africa, that is, in terms of its primacy. Freetown is approximately six times the size of the next largest urban center in the country. Not only is it the political capital, but it also dominates the economy of the country; it is the focus of the transportation system and by far the major port, and it rates an "index of modernization" five to ten times that of most other parts of the country.[8]

In another sense, however, Freetown is atypical of cities in West Africa, in that its origins are somewhat unique. The city was founded in 1787 as the site of a settlement for former slaves set free from England. After a difficult early period, the settlement grew in size, especially after 1808, when the British navy, operating from the Freetown harbor, captured slaving ships at sea and brought them to Freetown where the slaves were set free. Many remained, and the city steadily increased in size, such that there were over 18,000 inhabitants in 1848.[9]

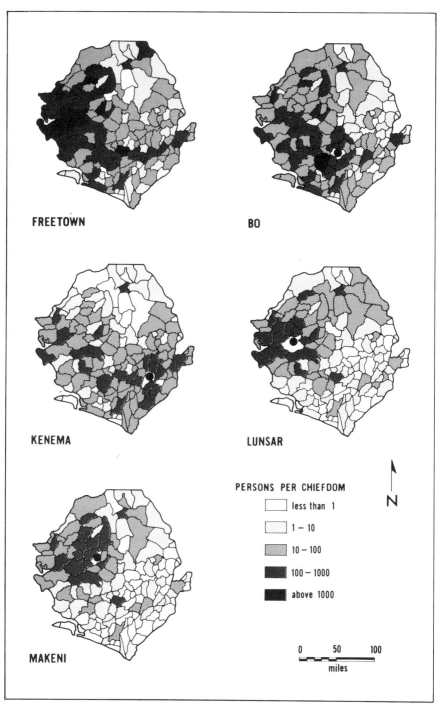

Figure 1. Cartographic portrayals of information collected by 1963 population census of Sierra Leone.

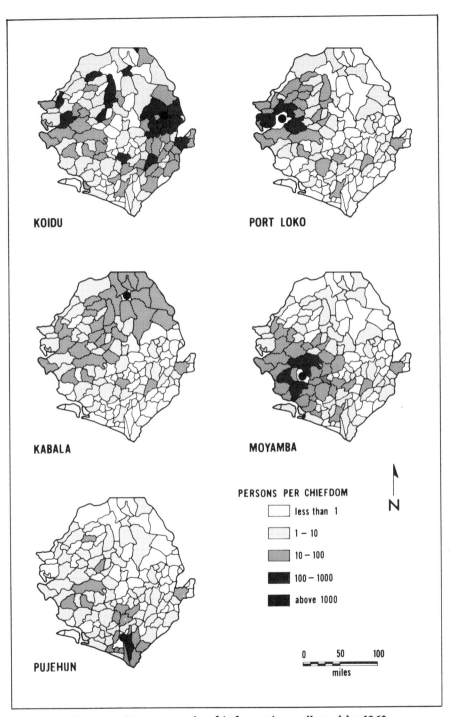

KOIDU

PORT LOKO

KABALA

MOYAMBA

PERSONS PER CHIEFDOM

less than 1

1 – 10

10 – 100

100 – 1000

above 1000

N

PUJEHUN

0   50   100

miles

Figure 2. Cartographic portrayals of information collected by 1963 population census of Sierra Leone.

As the city grew in size, it grew in attractiveness to the peoples of the hinterland, and by 1891 there were over 30,000 inhabitants, just over half of whom were descendants of the freed slaves. By 1901, the Creoles had lost their majority and by 1963, their plurality in the population, being swamped in numbers by the migration of the hinterland peoples. In fact, by the 1960s, Freetown was the largest agglomeration of virtually every tribal group of the Sierra Leone hinterland.

Fortunately for the analysis of this movement of people, the 1963 population census of Sierra Leone included a question on birthplace. The result was that for each administrative area, a numerical listing of the birthplace of the resident population was available and could be mapped.

Of the Freetown population providing satisfactory responses to the birthplace question (127,917), approximately one-third were born in chiefdoms outside of Freetown and its immediate surroundings. Their origins are diverse and include all but four of the chiefdoms (Figure 1). From this pattern, given the geographical conditions of the country, a set of suggestions regarding the areal variation in migration to the city is forthcoming. It includes

1. Distance decay effects. All other factors being held constant, there appears to be a regular decline in the numbers who have migrated to Freetown with the increase in distance from the city.
2. Transport influence. Those chiefdoms through which the railway runs have higher frequencies of migration than others in the same relative location, suggesting that early transport connection may be associated with a chainlike migration process (as discussed above).
3. Stepwise migration. The chiefdoms containing the largest provincial urban centers all generate many more migrants than those in the same relative location, and as they have been growing in size, they are both attracting and generating migrants according to the notions of stepwise migration (see "The Impact of the Colonial Period," above).
4. Land hunger and population pressure. These may be important factors, at least in the cases of several chiefdoms which have sent large numbers of migrants and are areas in which there are more people than the environmental base can support.
5. Alternative opportunities. Very few migrants to Freetown originate in the area proximate to the diamond fields in the eastern part of the country.

When these hypotheses are combined with those forces which have been identified as pushing people from the rural areas and pulling them toward urban centers, a set of hypotheses might be posited relating migration to Freetown to a set of variables with geographic expression. Such a migration model would incorporate seven generalized variables related to migration. These are

    (a) Distance decay
    (b) Population and population pressure
    (c) Education impact
    (d) Local urbanization in the sending area—urban effects
    (e) Traditional/modern local economic activity—local development
    (f) Alternative employment opportunities
    (g) Tribal or ethnic characteristics.[10]

Migration is the result of many factors. Perhaps at times these forces act separately; most often, they operate in combination. Thus, it is not suggested that the areal pattern of migration can be associated with any one of the above factors. Rather, migration to Freetown is expected to be the result of some combination of these forces. As yet, there is no suitable theory of migration which would suggest a set of variables which in combination would be associated with areal variations in migration to Freetown.

Thus, a migration model of the form

$$M_{ij} = f(X_a, X_b, X_c, X_d, X_e, X_f, X_g),$$

which simply says that migration is related in some fashion to the set of hypotheses a through g, above, is posited and related to the empirical data. Variables or hypotheses which add little or nothing to the explanation of varying migration propensities are successively eliminated until such time as a reduced model of the form

$$M_{ij} = f(X_a, X_d)$$

remains. This reduced set of explanatory variables explains the pattern of migration to Freetown in the most parsimonious fashion. Then, by interpreting this empirically derived model, one might make certain statements about the causes or determinants of migration to Freetown.

Two principal factors, when considered together, provide the best explanation of areal variations in migration to Freetown: distance decay and urbanization. No other hypotheses can compare with these factors in explaining the general pattern of urban-directed migration. One could predict the general level of urban-directed migration with a reasonable degree of accuracy from knowing the relative location of a chiefdom (in terms of its proximity to Freetown) and whether or not it included a provincial urban center. Those chiefdoms with urban places and in close proximity to the capital tend to send large numbers, while remote rural chiefdoms have had little migration contact. Ethnic group, educational experience, population pressure, and type of economic activity appear not to be related to the overall pattern of movement to Freetown, though this does not suggest that they might not be important in some areas or for some people. At the macro scale of analysis, any influence which these factors might have is overcome and masked by the two strong and dominating factors of relative proximity and the presence of a provincial urban place.[11]

Similar analyses of the nine other migration fields depicted in Figures 1 and 2 can also be conducted.[12] This group of urban centers is in no sense a random sample of towns in Sierra Leone, nor is it a systematic sample. Rather, the urban places have been chosen to represent the variety of urban situations which are available in terms of their locational attributes, ethnic environments, economic activities, and administrative importance. By so doing, one expects to tease out the level of importance such destination characteristics might have on the migration fields or upon the factors statistically related to migration to them.

A brief visual comparison indicates that each of the migration fields is unique in terms of location, areal extent, intensity of attraction, and eccentricity (or noncircularity). However, in every case, regardless of the attributes of the center of attraction, distance decay effects are visually apparent and dominate the spatial pattern of the field.

A statistical analysis of the migration fields, relating the intensity of migration to each of the urban centers from the surrounding chiefdoms to the set of hypothesized factors described above, was conducted. A summary of the general determinants of each of the ten migration fields is presented in Table 1. The explanatory factors statistically related to each of the migration fields are derived by reading across the rows; for example, migration to Moyamba is determined by distance decay (relative proximity) and urban effects (the stepwise migration of people up the urban hierarchy). It is important to indicate that the relative importance of the explanatory forces depicted in the table declines from left to right—Freetown's field, for example, is dominantly influenced by distance decay and then by urban effects. The next two explanatory variables are only very minor.

Thus, in eight of the nine cases, the spatial variation in the migration field is statistically explained by the two factors found to be so important in the case of Freetown—distance decay effects and urban influences. Chiefdoms in close proximity send more migrants to these centers, as do

Table 1. General Determinants of the Migration Fields

Center	Explanatory Factors			
Freetown	Distance decay	Urban effects	Alternative opportunity	Local development
Bo	Distance decay	Urban effects	Alternative opportunity	Education
Kenema	Distance decay	Urban effects	Alternative Opportunity	
Lunsar	Distance decay	Urban effects		
Makeni	Distance decay	Urban effects	Alternative opportunity	
Koidu	Distance decay	Urban effects	Modernization negative	Date connected
Port Loko	Distance decay			
Kabala	Distance decay	Urban effects		
Moyamba	Distance decay	Urban effects		

those with other small urban places included within their areas; areas far away and with little or no urbanization send few or no migrants. The only exception to this generalization is the town of Port Loko, which would have included urban effects if the statistical level had been only slightly reduced. The factors to the right-hand side of the table are relatively unimportant (though statistically significant) when compared to the two dominant explanatory forces. The alternative opportunity variable, which appears for four urban places, reflects the fact that in these cases the migrant fields are significantly affected by the location of the diamond fields as alternative employment opportunities.

In summary, it can be concluded from the results depicted in Table 1 that in terms of the data describing migration to urban centers from surrounding areas, the two forces of distance decay and urban effects dominate the explanation, regardless of the size, relative location, type of economic activity, level of administrative importance, or ethnic environment of the several urban centers.[13]

Notes

1. W. W. Rostow, *The Stages of Economic Growth* (Cambridge: Cambridge University Press, 1960.

2. J.B. Riddell, *The Spatial Dynamics of Modernization in Sierra Leone* (Evanston, Ill.: Northwestern University Press, 1970), pp. 61–71.

3. A. R. De Souza and P. W. Porter, *The Underdevelopment and Modernization of the Third World.* (Washington: Association of American Geographers, 1974).

4. S. Amin, ed., *Modern Migrations in West Africa.* (London: Oxford University Press, 1974).

5. M. P. Todaro, "A Model of Labor Migration and Urban Unemployment in Less Developed Countries," *American Economic Review* 59 (1969): 138–48.

6. This section draws heavily upon Riddell, *Spatial Dynamics.*

7. Figures 1 and 2 first appeared in J. B. Riddell, "Population Migration and Urbanization in Tropical Africa," *Pan-African Journal*, (1975).

8. Refer to the "Modernization Surface" map in Riddell, *Spatial Dynamics*, p. 91.

9. J. Peterson, *Province of Freedom* (Evanston, Ill.: Northwestern University Press, 1969).

10. These hypotheses are fully discussed in Riddell, *Spatial Dynamics*, pp. 107–14.

11. A more complete analysis may be found in J. B. Riddell, "On Structuring a Migration Mode," *Geographical Analysis* 2 (1970): 403–09.

12. See Riddell, "Population Migration," for a more complete analysis.

13. A concluding cautionary note should be sounded. These results apply only at the macro scale, and they do not allow for a precise differentiation between the person who migrates to an urban center and one who chooses not to migrate.

Richard W. Wilkie
and Jane Riblett Wilkie

Environmental Perception and Migration Behavior: A Case Study in Rural Argentina

Why is it that many migrants who leave remote rural villages to live in large, complex urban centers do so successfully and with relative ease, while others from the same village never really adjust to a complex environment, even after many years? Is it just native intelligence, or does it involve a broader perception and openness to the world that is reflected in such things as attitudes toward the environment and "mental maps" that each migrant has built up over time?

Clearly, the reasons for these differences involve complex interrelationships cutting across all components of human attitudes and behavior: psychological, socioeconomic, environmental, political, cultural, spatial, and others. While this chapter examines only environmental and spatial factors in depth, these are clearly not the only set of forces involved in this complex process. They do, however, prove to be contributing factors related to the ultimate success or lack of success in the assimilation into new environments for certain population subgroups from rural villages. Thus, for some migrants, these factors are the most important in explaining migration and assimilation behavior. For other migrants, who place low priority on environmental factors in decision-making, they have only minor influence. But most often, these forces operate indirectly to shape economic, social, and other decisions that relate to the migration process.

This chapter is a preliminary examination of how environmental and spatial perceptions and attitudes relate to migration from a rural village in Argentina. The village, Aldea San Francisco, is a Volga-Deutsch community of 236 inhabitants (1974) that is located in the province of Entre Rios.[1] With little industry, Entre Rios provided the second largest migration flow of any province to the capital city of Buenos Aires and its metropolitan area between 1947 and 1960. Aldea San Francisco is located with easy access to a wide range of urban-sized centers. The two largest metropolitan areas of Argentina, Gran Buenos Aires and Rosario, are 320 and 240 miles away, respectively, while within a 40-mile radius of the village are Santa Fé (250,000 population), Paraná (125,000), Diamante (13,000), and Crespo (7,600).

The village of Aldea San Francisco provides an instance to examine in depth both the migration process and changes in attitudes and village structures for the community of origin for two time periods, 1966–1967 and 1973–1974. In the latter time period, 247 out-migrants from the village were traced and interviewed in their new environments. The resulting data, collected both before and during the process of modernization in the village, permit both an analysis of rural modernization in its initial impact and a comparison of migrant and nonmigrant populations.

The Changing Argentine Urban–Rural Hierarchy

In Argentina, unlike many other Latin American countries where step-wise migration predominates, the largest shifts of population appear to be from rural areas of dispersed populations and small villages to large metropolitan centers of over half a million population. This was especially true between 1947 and 1960, but may have changed somewhat between 1960 and 1970 owing to the depletion of the rural dispersed population and the decline in rate of metropolitan growth. Figure 1 illustrates the changing percentages of population in each of five levels in the urban-rural hierarchy: *dispersed population* (1 to 200 population), *villages* (200 to 2,000), *simple urban centers* (2,000 to 20,000), *complex urban centers* (20,000 to 500,000), and *metropolitan areas* (over 500,000).[2]

In 1947, just under a third of the total population of Argentina lived in rural areas of dispersed population (29.5 percent), while an equal number lived in metropolitan areas (29.7 percent). The three middle community-size levels were underpopulated and contained just over a third of the population among them (villages, 7.7 percent; simple urban centers, 14.3 percent; and complex urban centers, 18.6 percent).[3] By 1960, the proportion of the population residing in the three middle levels was unchanged (up slightly, from 40.6 to 42.7 percent), the metropolitan level had gained significantly (from 29.8 to 40.2 percent), and the proportion of population dispersed fell by nearly half (down from 29.5 to 17.5 percent).[4] While the lack of net change in the proportion held by the middle levels may mask significant step and reverse migration, the most striking change between 1947 and 1960 was the movement directly out of dispersed and small-village zones to the largest urban centers.

The pattern of population change in the 1970s is not entirely clear. Published data from the Argentine census of 1970 show that metropolitan populations of over half a million continued to grow (up to 44.7 percent), but at a much reduced rate, less than half that of the prior decade.[5] Complex urban centers of between 20,000 and 500,000 population also increased their proportion of the total population (from 17.6 to 21.3 percent), while the three lowest levels all declined in proportion to the

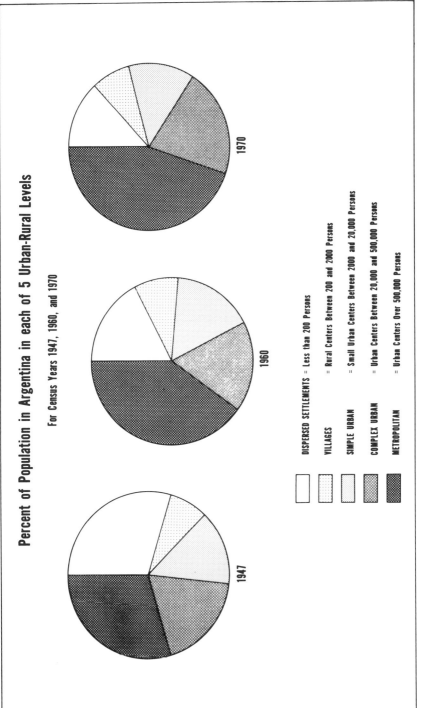

Percent of Population in Argentina in each of 5 Urban-Rural Levels

For Census Years 1947, 1960, and 1970

1970

1960

1947

DISPERSED SETTLEMENTS = Less than 200 Persons

VILLAGES = Rural Centers Between 200 and 2000 Persons

SIMPLE URBAN = Small Urban Centers Between 2000 and 20,000 Persons

COMPLEX URBAN = Urban Centers Between 20,000 and 500,000 Persons

METROPOLITAN = Urban Centers Over 500,000 Persons

Figure 1

Table 1. *Actual Location Versus Perceived Ideal Location—247 migrants from Aldea San Francisco, 1974 (in percents)*

	Actual Location			Ideal Location		
	total migrants n=247	males n=120	females n=127	total migrants n=232	males n=113	females n=119
Dispersed	11.3	14.2	8.7			
	17.8 <	20.0 <	15.8 <	27.5	41.6	17.6
Village	6.5	5.8	7.1			
Simple urban	32.8	35.8	29.9	14.2	19.5	10.9
Complex urban	15.4	10.0	20.5	20.2	17.7	25.2
Metropolitan	34.0	34.2	33.8	32.0	21.2	46.2
	100.0	100.0	100.0	100.0	100.0	100.0

total population. Simple urban centers declined from 16.0 to 13.1 percent, and village and dispersed populations (not separately reported) were reduced from a quarter (26.2 percent) to a fifth (20.9 percent) of the population.

Urban Hierarchy Location of Migrants from Aldea San Francisco

A comparison of actual urban-level destination of migrants from the study village with the size-of-place distribution of the Argentine population as a whole indicates strong similarities. In fact, the ideal location expressed by females is nearly identical with the current national distribution of population in the urban hierarchy (Table 1). Responses to a question on preferred location indicates that while over half of all migrants do not plan to move again in the near future, only a quarter of the males (25 percent) and about a third of the females (35 percent) would choose to remain in the particular urban or rural level in which they currently reside (Table 2).

Satisfaction with current location level and preferred city size differ significantly by sex. Among males, those in dispersed areas are the most satisfied, while for females, those in metropolitan areas are most satisfied. Dissatisfaction was highest among females in the dispersed and simple urban centers and among males in simple urban and metropolitan levels.

One additional observation on community-size selection stands out. Migration flows to various-sized urban communities reveal a pattern of movements that often bypass certain intervening cities. Many of the migrants making the first move passed through these centers on their way

Table 2. Current Location Compared with Perceived Ideal Location in the Urban Hierarchy—247 migrants from Aldea San Francisco, 1974 (in percents)

Currently living in	Ideally, would like to live in					
	Village-dispersed	Simple Urban	Complex Urban	Metro-politan	Total Percent	N
Dispersed 13.3	% satisf. 80	7	7	7	101	15
Village 6.2	% satisf. 14	57	29	0	100	7
Simple Urban 36.3	32	% satisf. 14	22	32	100	41
Complex urban 8.8	40	10	% satisf. 20	30	100	10
Metropolitan 35.4	42	25	15	% satisf. 18	100	40
				overall satisfaction 25%		
Total percent preferring each level	42	19	18	21	100	
N =	47	22	20	24		113 (7 males had no opinion)

MALES

to either Gran Buenos Aires or other distant points. The nearby complex urban centers of Paraná and Santa Fé and the metropolitan center of Rosario together received less than 7 percent of all migrants by 1966 and just over 8 percent by 1975. While many of these centers have job opportunities similar to those in Gran Buenos Aires, they did not attract many migrants from Aldea San Francisco, and the few they did attract were predominately lower-class women who became private-household workers. Rosario, Argentina's second largest city, attracted only four migrants, and Santa Fé, the fifth largest city, attracted none until the early 1970s. Clearly, for most migrants from the village, other forces are playing a more important role in their migration decisions than are ease of access to or prior knowledge of nearby large urban centers.

FEMALES

Currently living in	Ideally, would like to live in					
	Village-dispersed	Simple Urban	Complex Urban	Metro-politan	Total Percent	N
Dispersed 7.6	% satisf. 11	22	56	11	100	9
Village 6.7	% satisf. 50	0	0	50	100	8
Simple urban 30.3	11	% satisf. 17	33	39	100	36
Complex urban 8.8	16	16	% satisf. 24	44	100	25
Metropolitan	20	2	17	% satisf. 61	100	41
Total percent preferring each level	18	11	25	overall satisfaction 35 46	100	
N =	21	13	30	55		119 (8 females had no opinion)

Environmental Attitudes and the Migration Process

While more than fifty variables related to spatial and environmental attitudes and perception were collected in the study, only three are examined here: (a) age of child exploration of the village region, (b) trust versus mistrust of the physical environment, and (c) use versus preservation of environmental resources.

CHILD EXPLORATION OF THE ENVIRONMENT

Probably every child, when faced with the problem of whether the environment will respond adequately to his expression of his needs, asks himself: How can I

Table 3.   Percent of Child Exploration Age Groups in Each Urban Level
After First Move from Aldea San Francisco, 1966—Mothers'
attitudes toward age of child exploration of neighborhood up to 2
to 3 kms.

Level migrants Living after First Move	Early: under age 6	Medium Early: ages 6 to 8	Medium Late: ages 9 to 12	Late: ages 13 to 18	Total Migrants (n=139)
Village-dispersed under 2,000	25	30	30	47	34
Simple urban 2,000—19,999	11	13	40	16	17
Complex urban 20,000—500,000	14	4	4	11	9
Metropolitan over 500,000	50	52	26	26	40
Total percent	100	100	100	100	100
Percent of total in each group	20	33	20	27	100

Chi-square: $p < .001$

best assure that my needs will be fulfilled adequately? What can I learn from my
experiences? How can I find order in my universe?

—Everett Hagen, *On the Theory of Social Change*

A whole constellation of child-rearing practices has been established as
playing an important role in shaping the attitudes and behavior of
individuals. Several writers have found that the age of children at which
parents encourage independence plays a key role in children's understanding of causal relationships and ultimately in the formation of a trust in
both themselves and the social and physical environment around them.[6]
Child exploration of the neighborhood and region up to two to three
kilometers is one element of this independence training. In an earlier study
of migrants from Aldea San Francisco, it was found that age of exploration (as expressed by the parents) was associated with destination community size of migrants.[7] Those who located in the most rural level were in
the latest age group allowed to explore the area up to three kilometers
around Aldea San Francisco. Nearly half (47 percent) of this late exploration group moved to other small villages or dispersed rural landscapes
(Table 3). The medium-late exploration group moved to slightly more
urban levels, with 40 percent going to simple urban centers but nearly a

third moving to other rural areas. In the medium-early exploration group, slightly over half (52 percent) moved to the most complex metropolitan centers.

The age between six and eight has been described by David McClelland as being most crucial for the child to receive encouragement for autonomous decision-making if that child is to internalize the ability to understand complex relationships. This age is neither too early for the child's abilities nor too late for the child to internalize standards as his or her own. This study shows that children encouraged to explore the neighborhood autonomously between ages six and eight were ultimately drawn to the most complex urban level in the hierarchy. Finally, among children who had the freedom to explore exceptionally early, before age six, there was a slight drop in the percentage going to metropolitan urban levels, although this level still accounted for half the destinations of this group on the first move; and a higher proportion than other groups moved to the complex urban level of cities between 20,000 and half a million population (Table 3).

TRUST VERSUS MISTRUST OF THE PHYSICAL ENVIRONMENT

If a child explores the neighborhood and the physical environment around the home community and gains both an understanding of the complexities of the physical and spatial systems and a trust in his or her own abilities to understand them, this trust is later transferred to the physical environment. Children whose explorations are overly restricted and controlled and who do not gain an understanding of these systems or of their own abilities to control and work with the environment often develop a mistrust and fear of the physical world. This fear and mistrust of the environment has been described by Everett Hagen:

> These perceptions breed in him a fear of using his initiative, an
> uncertainty concerning the quality of his judgment, a tendency
> to let someone else evaluate a situation in order to avoid frustra-
> tion and anxiety. Out of these perceptions also grows un-
> easiness at facing unresolved situations. Rather than rely on
> his own analysis to solve problems of the physical world or his
> relations to other individuals, he avoids pain by falling back on
> traditional ways of behavior that his parents and other earlier
> authorities taught him, and by relying on the judgment or will
> of individuals superior to him in authority or power. . . . In other
> matters—storm, drought, the run of fish in the fishing grounds;
> death of his crops, his cattle, his kin—he knows that no direct

actions of his will bring him security or save him from disaster. He knows that events have causes, and he attributes these events, whose causes are forces he cannot see, to the will of unseen forces. By magic or some equivalent he seeks to induce the spiritual forces to befriend rather than harm him. In some cultures great stress is placed on living in harmony with the universe so good may come; in others appeasement or bribing of the spirits is stressed.[8]

Four different approaches were used to measure this abstract sense of trust or mistrust as it relates to the natural environment. All villagers and all migrants were asked directly, in two separate questions, to scale how strongly they felt trust or mistrust in the natural environment. In addition, they were asked to score sixteen environmental hazards as to how much they worried about or were preoccupied with the threat of each hazard (migrants scored only seven environmental hazards). Finally, in both the earlier village study in 1966–1967 and the later study in 1973–1974, trust versus mistrust of the environment was indexed by scoring the total number of positive and/or negative statements concerning the environment in more than fifteen open-ended questions defining "the good life," good and bad things about Aldea San Francisco and the migrant location, job and life satisfaction, and others. The analysis used in this chapter contrasts the village and migrant populations by sex and urban level on one of the two direct questions (Figure 2).[9]

Overall, the village population expressed greater trust in the environment than did the migrant population ("some trust" was the village mean and "a little trust" was the migrant mean). Males in both groups have the highest overall scores, and about half the males in each group have "complete trust" in the physical environment. Females in Aldea San Francisco generally lead a more controlled and restricted life, and this appears in their higher sense of environmental fear. The village female subgroup had nearly the same mean score as the migrant male subgroup, but only a fourth of them expressed "complete confidence" in the physical environment. The migrant female subgroup expressed the greatest mistrust of all groups; a fifth said they had "some fear," and nearly a fourth stated that they had "much fear" of the physical environment.

Higher trust in the physical environment undoubtedly contributed to the male migrants' desire to live in rural areas (47 percent preferred locations either in villages or dispersed on the landscape), just as females' higher mistrust contributed to their preference for either metropolitan centers (55 percent) or complex urban centers (30 percent).

A contradiction appears to exist, however. Environmental fear is highest among the subgroup of metropolitan female migrants, who expressed the greatest satisfaction with their current location in the urban hierarchy.

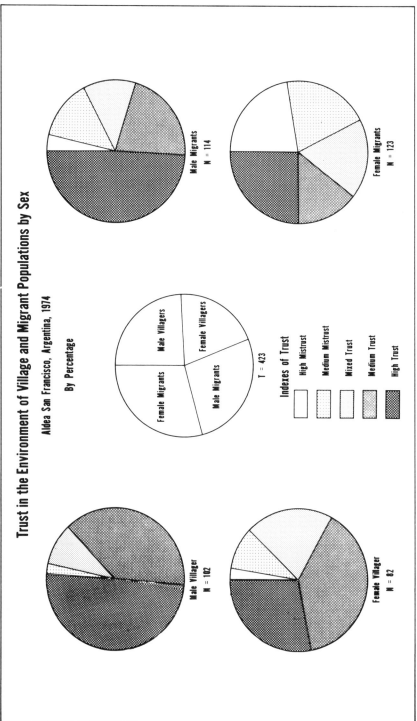

Figure 2

This seems inconsistent with the previous findings that earlier child exploration leads to higher trust in the environment and in the ability to understand and cope with complex systems. In fact, there are two distinct groups of female migrants from Aldea San Francisco in metropolitan areas. The first group includes that half of all metropolitan female migrants who have lower social class origins in the village and who overwhelmingly score high in environmental mistrust (only 20 percent have "some" or "complete confidence" in the physical environment). This group moves to metropolitan areas like Buenos Aires primarily out of economic necessity and is often unprepared for life there. Lower-class children in the village often explore the environment too early or too late, score lower in environmental trust, and are more oriented to tradition and reliance on the decisions of others.[10] The women are not well assimilated into their new urban social environments either, since 70 percent of those who expressed "some" or "much fear" in the physical environment said they have "nothing in common with their neighbors" and are not in reality part of the community.

The second group of female migrants to metropolitan areas, on the other hand, does fit the previous model. These are mostly females with middle-class origins who explored the environment moderately early, have higher trust in the environment, and moved to the largest and most complex urban centers in the nation for social and psychological reasons. Thus, metropolitan areas attract those migrants most capable as well as those least capable of assimilating and doing well in very complex situations.[11]

For some migrants, mistrust of the environment decreases in the move from a village to complex urban and metropolitan centers. Douglas Butterworth explains this with regard to rural Oaxacan migrants living in Mexico City:

> In Mexico City, the migrants say they have "lost the fear" which they had in Tilantongo. No longer are they servile creatures of the whims of the "bad elements" (*malos elementos*) in their community, human and natural. . . . They have lost "the fear" of the ever-present possibility that the natural elements can, and often do, wipe out a year's food supply.[12]

While the environment of the Entre Rios agricultural region that includes Aldea San Francisco is not nearly as harsh as that of Oaxaca (and the social situation is more peaceful), environmental hazards such as drought are common. This, along with the unfavorable price structure for agriculture and other rural problems, contributes to a sense of fear that seems to be most profound among selected females. These women opt for a new life in the least natural and most human-controlled environment of all—complex urban and metropolitan areas.

The final environmental concept to be examined in this chapter contrasts attitudes of villagers and migrants toward the development of natural resources. Is it more important to develop and use the environmental resources now, or is it more important to preserve and protect them in order to prevent an unknown environmental crisis in the future?

The desire for human dominance and control over nature and the environment has been a universal theme. Until recently, it was generally thought that environmental resources were endless, and little concern was given to their preservation and careful control. In much of Latin America, environmental preservation is still an alien concept. While both villagers and migrants from Aldea San Francisco readily understood the concept and in most cases had well-developed thoughts on the subject, many Argentine urbanites with little environmental contact in their past had trouble understanding that there are two positions on the question.[13] In this study, the villagers and migrants were asked to select either one position or the other, but only the village population was asked to score how strongly they felt on the subject.

The results of this question vary greatly by sex and age, as well as by village and migrant subgroups (Figures 3 and 4). Age differences appear to reflect changes in attitudes that correspond to the life cycle and are different for males and females. In their early years, both sex groups favor environmental preservation, with the exception of male migrants. By age thirty, all groups are predominantly for preservation and continue to be so until age forty, except for village males, who are strongly in favor of using the environment until their early forties. During their late twenties and thirties, village males take on family responsibilities and establish their agricultural careers within the environment. At that time they revert back to stronger feelings toward using the environment during their declining years. Village females seem to become the driving force in many families between ages forty and fifty and then revert to their prior pattern of environmental preservation. Migrant populations consistently support the concept of environmental preservation throughout their lives, with only two exceptions. Village males start low and continue to rise until at age seventy, nearly 90 percent are for preservation, while female migrants start high and by age seventy end up nearly equally divided on the question.

The urbanization experience appears to lead to a greater feeling of

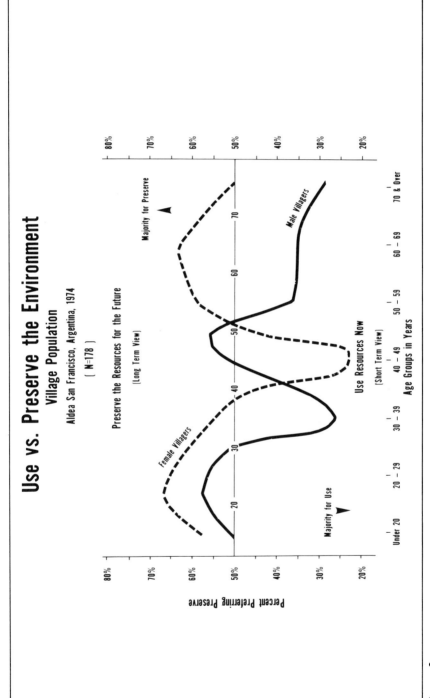

Figure 3

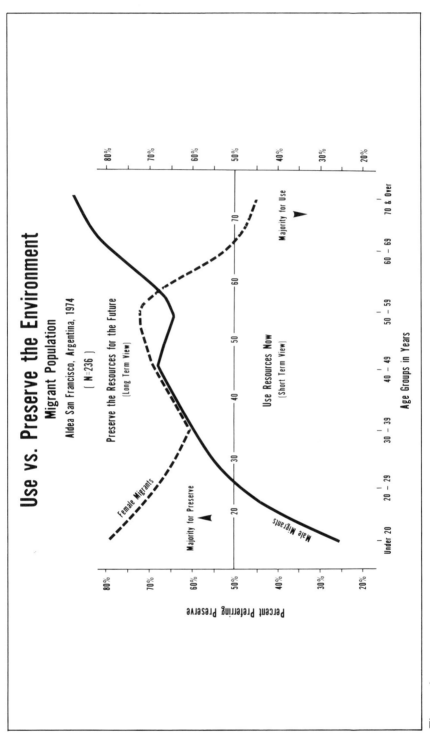

Figure 4

environmental concern among exruralists. Overall, nearly two-thirds of all migrants (63.2 percent), express a greater need for environmental preservation, while slightly less than half of the total village population (47.8 percent) feels the same way. Among villagers, the strongest push for environmental dominance comes in the middle years and again near the end of the life cycle. Villagers live much closer to nature and have to face the day-to-day reality of making a living from the environment; on the other hand, the migrant population has (generally) removed itself from the closeness to nature, and a greater sense of an idealized view of nature begins to emerge as it faces a declining environmental quality in the cities.[14]

Conclusions

An examination of three environmental and spatial attitudes has shown that they contribute to three particular kinds of migration factors: (a) size of the destination community, (b) satisfaction with that particular size level in the urban-rural hierarchy, and (c) level of neighborhood (social) assimilation in the new locations. Earlier child exploration relates to movement to larger urban centers, while late exploration leads to moves to smaller centers. A higher trust in the environment leads to fewer problems in assimilation into more complex environments, but also for most males contributes to a desire to live in smaller communities closer to nature, and for most females, to a desire to live in large urban centers where they experience a less restrictive social environment. Attitudes toward use versus preservation of the environment vary by sex and age in the life cycle. Furthermore, these attitudes show a greater tendency for preservation the longer a migrant has been away from the village.

While a conceptual model specifying the relationships between environmental attitudes and spatial behavior has not been fully developed here, the role of attitudes in migrant destination decisions has been established. These relationships may vary among cultures, by levels of economic development and ecological sensitivity in societies, and over time, but until more case studies that measure comparable dimensions of environmental attitudes and behavior are completed, it will not be possible to establish the universality of these observations.[15]

Notes

* This research was supported by a grant from the National Institute of Child Health and Human Development (Project No. HDO7397).

1. "Volga-Deutsch" defines German Catholics who moved in large numbers to the central Volga River region of Russia in the 1760s under Catherine the Great and then to Argentina in the late 1870s.
2. For a detailed discussion of the selection of these five urban-rural levels, see Richard W. Wilkie, "Urban Growth and the Transformation of the Settlement Landscape of Mexico: 1910–1970 in *Contemporary Mexico*, James Wilkie, Michael Meyer, and Edna Monzon de Wilkie, eds. (Proceedings of the IV International Congress of Mexican Studies, Berkeley and Mexico: University of California Press and El Colegio de Mexico, in press 1976), pp. 99–134.
3. *IV Censo de la Nación: Argentina 1947* (Buenos Aires: Dirección Nacional del Servicio Estadístico).
4. *Censo Nacional de Población: 1960* (Buenos Aires: Dirección Nacional de Estadística y Censos).
5. *Censo Nacional de Población, Familias y Viviendas— 1970: Resultos Provisionales* (Buenos Aires: Instituto Nacional de Estadística y Censos).
6. For a representative sample of this literature, see Erik Erickson, *Childhood and Society* (New York: Norton, 1950); Everett Hagen, *On the Theory of Social Change* (Homewood, Ill.: Dorsey Press, 1962); David McClelland, *The Achieving Society* (Princton, N.J.: Van Nostrand, 1958); Michael Southworth, "Cambridgeport Boys' Conception and Use of the City" (Ph.D. diss., Massachusetts Institute of Technology, 1970); and Marion Winterbottom, "The Relation of Need for Achievement to Learning Experience in Independence and Mastery," in *Motives in Fantasy, Action, and Society*, J. W. Atkinson, ed. (Princeton, N.J.: Van Nostrand, 1958), pp. 453–78.
7. Richard Wilkie, "Rural Depopulation: A Case Study of an Argentine Village" (Paper presented to the International Biological Programme V General Assembly, September 1972), forthcoming in *Proceedings of the IBP V General Assembly*, Everett Lee, ed. (London: Oxford University Press, in press 1976).
8. Hagen, *On the Theory of Social Change,* pp. 69–70 and 97.
9. That is, "With respect to nature and the physical environment, what kind of a person would you say that you are? A person with: (1) much fear of nature and the physical environment, (2) some fear, (3) a little fear, (4) a little confidence, (5) some confidence, or (6) complete confidence in nature and the physical environment?"
10. The migration process from Aldea San Francisco for the 1966–1967 period by social class and sex is described in Richard Wilkie, "Toward a Behavioral Model of Peasant Migration: An Argentine Case of Spatial Behavior by Social Class Level," in *Population Dynamics of Latin America*, Robert N. Thomas, ed. (East Lansing, Mich.: CLAG Publications, 1972), pp. 83–114.
11. In the 1966–1967 study, it was found that two-thirds (66 percent) of the migrants coming from families with high ambition scores moved to metropolitan areas, but so did half (47 percent) of all those with high scores of resignation to fate. Those with mixed scores of ambition and resignation

moved (in nine cases out of ten) to middle and lower levels of the urban hierarchy. A discussion of how metropolitan areas draw those most capable as well as those least capable is found in Richard Wilkie, "Rural Depopulation," p. 19.

12. Douglas S. Butterworth, "A Study of the Urbanization Process among Mixtec Migrants from Tilantogo in Mexico City," *América Indígena* 22, no. 3 (Julio 1962): 271.

13. One knowledgeable Argentine social scientist expressed the idea that to use and to preserve are the same thing. She stated that if one is preserving an environmental resource, it means that one owns it (why else would anyone preserve it?), and one can use it as rapidly or as slowly as one wishes because it belongs to one. She refused to acknowledge that the public sector has certain environmental rights and needs, and she could only relate to the concept from a personal point of view. Clearly, she would have scored very high on the "use" end of the scale since her idea was to exploit the environment. A recent paper by Robert Claxton, "Environmental Concern in Latin America," presented to the 1975 annual meeting of the Georgia Academy of Science, pointed out that environmentalism in Latin America is weak and limited to elite circles and that most Latin American leaders actually fear any form of environmentalism that would limit their attempts to develop.

14. While these facts are not explored here, it should be noted that although individuals who have high trust in the environment also opt for environmental preservation, there is a subgroup that trusts the environment because it is using it successfully, as well as another small subgroup that says it fears the environment, which should be preserved so it will not strike back at these people (appeasement of the gods).

15. For a detailed description of the process methodology used in this study that looks at changes over time in behavioral-level case studies, see Richard W. Wilkie, "The Process Method versus The Hypothesis Method: A Nonlinear Example of Peasant Spatial Perception and Behavior," in *Proceedings of the 1972 Meeting of the International Geographical Commission on Quantitative Geography*, Maurice Yeates, ed. (Montreal and London: McGill-Queen's University Press, 1974), pp. 1–31.

Bernard Gallin
and Rita S. Gallin

The Integration of Village Migrants into Urban Society: The Case of Taipei, Taiwan *

The island of Taiwan lies astride the Tropic of Cancer in the East China Sea, some one hundred miles off the coast of China. Traditionally, Taiwan and China shared common social and political institutions that were reflections of their agrarian-based societies, in which commerce and industry played only a small role. In the past two-and-a-half decades, however, Taiwan (the Republic of China) and the People's Republic of China have drifted apart, each taking different roads to development.

Taiwan today is facing some critical choices for its future development. Agricultural policies are central to economic planning and have significant implications in the social and political realm as well. High farm productivity must be maintained or even increased. Food is needed to feed an increasingly nonagricultural population, and capital is needed to subsidize growing industrialization. Neither food nor capital, however, can continue to be extracted from an agricultural system based on a traditional technology. Moreover, cultivators will continue to give up working the land if their profits remain low. Despite the remarkable record of Taiwan's economic achievements, therefore, agriculture in Taiwan—particularly the cultivation of rice, the island's most important food crop—is and has been in a state of near crisis for several years.

On the other hand, industrial productivity in Taiwan has grown enormously over the past twenty years. Between the early 1950s and 1966, industrial productivity more than quadrupled, and between 1960 and 1966, it more than doubled. During these same years, agricultural productivity increased by approximately 45 percent. In the years since, although industrial productivity has continued to rise, agricultural productivity has not. In both 1969 and 1971, it fell below the 1966 baseline figure, and during other years it rose only slightly.

These differing growth rates reflect the development policies adopted by the Nationalist government. Industrial development has been financed (a) by capital extracted from the agricultural sector of the population, and (b) by foreign capital lured to the island by its relatively stable economic and political situation. It has been fueled by human capital drawn from the island's rural villages and smaller towns and cities.

On the one hand, the rural-to-urban flow has been stimulated by conditions in the city such as employment opportunities in business, factories, and service, which have burgeoned since the early stages of Taiwan's industrialization. On the other hand, the flow of rural inhabitants has been encouraged by conditions in the countryside such as overpopulation, landlessness, family farms far too small to support all family members, and general rural underemployment.

Rural-to-urban migration in Taiwan, however, is hardly a new phenomenon, nor is it a consequence only of rural economic pressures. The proportion of Taiwanese living in cities rose from 10.5 percent in 1920 to 15.2 percent in 1950 and 24.4 percent in 1966.[1] Natural increase accounts for part of this growth, but migration has played the major role, for fertility rates are lower in the cities than in the countryside.[2] As of 1956, fully one-third of the residents of the island's two largest cities were Taiwanese in-migrants.[3]

The subject here is a subset of these rural-to-urban migrants. First, we briefly examine the differences between migrants whose destination is a nearby city and those headed for more distant urban centers and distinguish these out-migrants from nonmigrants in their native villages. We deal specifically with natives of four primarily agricultural villages—Hsin-hsing, Ta-yu, Yung-p'ing, and P'u-yen—all situated in P'u-yen *hsiang,* a rural township in Chang-hua county approximately 130 miles from Taipei in the west-central coastal plain of Taiwan. Data for this discussion have been drawn from the official household record books *(hu-k'ou)* maintained in the P'u-yen township public office.[4]

We are mainly interested in long-distance migrants to Taipei, concentrating on Hsin-hsing villagers with whom we have worked in three field studies, in the village, in the more extended local territorial system to which the village belongs, and in the city. Our purpose is to show how these migrants relate economically and sociopolitically to the urban situation and how their network of relationships, especially those based on kinship, village, and occupational ties, affect their integration into Taipei life.

Out-Migration From Hsin-hsing and Three Other Villages

The four villages in question were all originally settled in the late eighteenth century by Hokkien immigrants from the coastal region of southern Fukien; Hsin-hsing, with a resident population in 1970 of 580, is the smallest and also the poorest of the four villages. The registered popula-

Table 1. Out-Migration in Four Taiwanese Villages, 1945–1970

Village of Origin

Destination or Category of Migrants	Hsin-hsing No.	%	Yung-p'ing No.	%	Ta-yu No.	%	P'u-yen No.	%
Taipei	266	28.1	252	14.9	196	8.9	167	9.0
Keelung	—	—	—	—	53	2.4	—	—
Kaohsiung (including Tainan)	54	5.7	8	0.5	51	2.3	78	4.2
Total long-distance stream (Taipei, Keelung, Kaohsiung)	320	33.8	260	15.4	300	13.6	245	13.3
Taichung and Chang-hua	—	—	22	1.3	28	1.3	86	4.6
Nearby market towns	47	5.0	80	4.7	135	6.1	151	8.1
Total short-distance stream (Taichung, Chang-hua, nearby towns)	47	5.0	102	6.0	163	7.4	237	12.7
Total out-migrants, both streams	367	38.8	362	21.5	463	21.0	482	25.9
Total registered population, 1970	580	61.2	1,325	78.5	1,742	79.0	1,378	74.1
Total living population originally registered in the village	947	100.0	1,687	100.0	2,205	100.0	1,860	100.0

Source: Here and for all the tables in this chapter, unless otherwise noted, the source is the household record book *(hu-k'ou)*, 1970, in the public office of P'u-yen township.

tions of Ta-yu, Yung-p'ing, and P'u-yen, numbering 1,742, 1,325, and 1,378 respectively as of 1970, are on the average somewhat more prosperous and better educated than those of Hsin-hsing. Only P'u-yen has any local industry; as the seat of the township, it also houses the public office, farmers' association, and health station.

Residents have been emigrating from all four villages for more than twenty years. In Hsin-hsing, this emigration has resulted in large part from the growing intensity of population pressure on the land. This problem has been less severe in the other three villages, and as a consequence, emigration began somewhat later there and has progressed at a slower rate than in Hsin-hsing. The proportion of Hsin-hsing villagers who have emigrated since the mid-1940s is 38.8 percent of the combined total of the number of people currently registered as village residents and the number recorded as having moved. The comparable statistic for the other three villages combined is 22.7 percent—still a sizable proportion (Table 1).

Despite these different migration rates, emigration from all four villages has followed similar patterns; certain types of people have migrated to certain types of localities. Furthermore, it is useful to distinguish two streams of migrants. One consists of villagers who have moved short distances to local towns or to the nearby cities. The second stream consists of villagers who have traveled to larger, more distant cities, in particular to the industrial centers of Taipei (including such de facto suburbs as San-chung municipality and Pan-ch'iao township), Keelung, and Kaohsiung. The second stream is by far the larger of the two. About 87 percent of the migrants from Hsin-hsing, 72 percent of those from Ta-yu, 65 percent of those from Yung-p'ing, and 51 percent of those from P'u-yen traveled to the larger, more distant cities.

SHORT-DISTANCE MIGRATION

The two streams differ in several respects. Those who migrate only a short distance tend to come from families of comparatively high socioeconomic status. Generally, they have ample landholdings, surplus capital, or both, and family members are not tied to the land. A frequent purpose of local migration is to diversify their economic base.

Males who migrate short distances are usually married at the time of migration (or at least by the time the move is registered at the local public office). On the whole, they are also better educated than migrants who move longer distances. Table 2 shows a distinct preference of villagers with a junior- or senior-high-school education for local as opposed to long-distance migration.

For the most part, short-distance migrants engage in some kind of small business or small-scale manufacturing, work as technicians or craftsmen, or are employed as professionals or civil servants. Very few become laborers or unskilled workers. In large part, then, they are upwardly mobile, and they view the urban places nearby as more advantageous than the distant urban centers. In the nearby places, they have relationships with people who can help them achieve their social and economic goals. In addition, those migrants who attempt some new business generally find the competition less intense in local towns and in the slower-growing nearby cities than in Taipei and Kaohsiung, and therefore these places appear better suited to their sometimes limited business experience. At the same time, since some of these local migrants continue to maintain significant landholdings in their home village, moving to such nearby areas makes returning home when they must care for their land or attend to village affairs relatively easy.

Table 2. Educational Level of Male Emigrants and Nonmigrants Aged 15–59 for Four Taiwanese Villages, 1945–1970

Village of Origin and Migratory Category	Illiterate	Educational Attainment				
		Literate (no formal schooling)	Primary Schooling	Junior High	Senior High	Total
Hsin-hsing:						
Long-distance migrants	18.1%	3.2%	64.9%	7.4%	6.4%	100.0%
Short-distance migrants	14.3	—	57.1	14.3	14.3	100.0
Nonmigrants	15.3	8.3	56.3	10.4	9.7	100.0
Yung-p'ing:						
Long-distance migrants	26.1	—	62.5	5.7	5.7	100.0
Short-distance migrants	15.4	7.7	34.6	11.5	30.8	100.0
Nonmigrants	16.1	5.4	59.7	12.4	6.5	100.0
Ta-yu:						
Long-distance migrants	23.4	2.1	66.0	5.3	3.2	100.0
Short-distance migrants	23.1	5.1	56.4	5.1	10.3	100.0
Nonmigrants	17.5	3.0	63.3	9.5	6.7	100.0
P'u-yen:						
Long-distance migrants	19.8	1.2	62.8	8.1	8.1	100.0
Short-distance migrants	8.5	5.1	54.2	13.6	18.6	100.0
Nonmigrants	17.1	3.1	55.8	18.1	5.9	100.0

Note: By "short-distance" is meant migration to localities in Chang-hua county, T'ai-chung county, and Taichung municipality. "Long-distance" refers to migration to all other localities in Taiwan. In practice, destinations are limited to Kaohsiung and Tainan municipalities to the south and to greater Taipei, including Keelung and San-chung municipalities to the north. The figures for nonmigrants refer only to people registered *and* resident in the village during 1970.

LONG-DISTANCE MIGRATION

That the great majority of migrants from these four villages go to large cities rather than to less urbanized townships is exceptional for Taiwan as a whole. In 1967, proportionately more migrants from rural townships such as P'u-yen moved to urban townships than to large cities (Table 3).[5] It seems clear, then, that the largest cities are most attractive to migrants with little capital and few skills, for only there can they find relatively high-paying employment. Thus, among the four villages in question, the big-city, long-distance migration stream predominates most strongly (87 percent) in Hsin-hsing, the poorest, and least strongly (51 percent) in P'u-yen, the richest.

Table 3. Direction of Migration in Taiwan, 1967

Origin and Destination	Estimated Gross Migration (in thousands)
Large cities to	
Large cities	42.3
Urban townships and small cities	75.5
Rural townships	46.8
Total	164.6
Urban townships and small cities to	
Large cities	107.9
Urban townships	103.7
Rural townships	92.9
Total	304.5
Rural townships to	
Large cities	75.9
Urban townships and small cities	105.4
Rural townships	72.9
Total	254.2
Overall total	723.3

Source: Alden Speare, Jr., "The Determinants of Rural-to-Urban Migration in Taiwan" (Ph.D, diss., University of Michigan, 1969), p. 45, Table 3.1.
Note: Figures here include both mainlanders and Taiwanese.

Until very recently, P'u-yen township had no local industries and few job opportunities. Even today, such industries as do exist pay far lower wages than do their counterparts in Taipei, Keelung, and Kaohsiung. In general, local towns and cities have had relatively little to offer villagers with limited capital, poor education, undeveloped skills, and networks of relationships with people of similar limited backgrounds. In these circumstances, and given the fine transportation system in Taiwan, it is not surprising that a high proportion of poorer emigrants from the four villages head for the largest cities. The discussion that follows focuses on the eighty-four Hsin-hsing males who emigrated to Taipei.

Hsin-hsing migrants began moving to Taipei in 1945, and the flow continues. The earliest period, 1945–1950, saw the heaviest migration, namely 44 percent of the male population. These earliest migrants were older and more often married at the time they moved than were those who followed in later decades. During the 1950s and 1960s, the flow to Taipei tapered off slightly, and migrants were more often single and young (Table 4).

The families of Hsin-hsing migrants own less land on the average than

Table 4. Marital Status at the Time of Migration for Male Migrants from Hsin-hsing to Taipei, 1945–1970

Marital Status	Years of Migration			
	1945–50	1951–60	1961–69	Total
Married persons:				
Number	20	7	8	35
Percent	54.1	26.9	38.1	41.7
Single persons:				
Number	17	19	13	49
Percent	45.9	73.1	61.9	58.3
Total number	37	26	21	84
Persons under 17 at the time of migration:				
Number	11	15	9	35
Percent	29.7	57.7	42.9	41.7

Source: As in other tables, plus interviews.

Table 5. Landholding in Hsin-hsing of Male Migrants to Taipei at the Time of Migration, 1941–1969

Landholdings	Years of Migration			
	1945–50	1951–60	1961–69	Total
Total number of migrants	37	26	21	84
Migrants without land:				
Number	10	9	4	23
Percent of all migrants	27.0	34.6	19.0	27.4
Migrants with land:				
Number	27	17	17	61
Percent of all migrants	73.0	65.4	81.0	72.6
Landholdings (*chia*):				
Total owned land	7.27	8.32	5.89	21.48
Average owned land	0.27	0.49	0.35	0.35
Total tenanted land	3.91	2.46	3.22	9.59
Average tenanted land	0.14	0.14	0.19	0.16
Average total holding	0.41	0.63	0.54	0.51

Source: Interviews and land records of the Land Bureau of Chang-hua county.
Note: 1 *chia* = 2.39 acres.

*Table 6. Occupations of male migrants from Hsin-hsing upon arrival in
Taipei, 1945-70.*

Occupations	Related to activities in the Taipei Central Market	Unrelated to the Taipei Central Market	Total
Cart driver (laborer)	30	4	34
Pedicab driver	0	7	7
Manual worker	1	0	1
Shop clerk	13	2	15
Factory worker	0	3	3
Vegetable gardener	2	0	2
Apprentice	0	4	4
Servant	0	2	2
Sanitation worker	0	1	1
Carpenter	0	4	4
Technician	0	1	1
Peddler	3	3	6
Shopkeeper (merchant)	4	0	4
Total	53	31	84
Percent	63.1%	36.9%	100%

Source: Field interviews.
Note: The manual worker was an unskilled laborer working for a construction company.
The terms cart driver/laborer are used interchangeably throughout the text.

do villagers in Taiwan as a whole and significantly less than the average
Hsin-hsing resident whose family members have not migrated. Table 5
shows a significant difference between the 1945–1950 and 1951–1960
cohorts in the average size of landholding. It should be noted, however,
that many migrants, particularly the young single men who are more
prominent in the second cohort, come from lineal families whose holdings
have not yet been divided between the migrant and his brother(s).

Hsin-hsing migrants to Taipei have generally poor education backgrounds. Their educational level is lower than that of Hsin-hsing villagers
who do not migrate or who migrate to nearby towns and cities (Table 2).
In keeping with their low level of educational attainment, the majority
worked as laborers on their arrival in Taipei (Table 6). Over time, a few
became shopkeepers. Others became clerks in the Central Market, but a
significant proportion of these quit to become laborers because of the
higher pay. In any case, the majority of the men from Hsin-hsing, and
from the other three villages as well, became laborers when they arrived in
Taipei, and a majority are laborers even today.

Most long-distance migrants perceive their move as one of economic necessity, although in a strict sense this is by no means the case. Some migrants are from families whose landholdings were adequate for their needs. Others are from large families that wanted to diversify their economic resources or supplement their income. Perhaps, too, a certain amount of venturesomeness played a part in the decision to move; the city pulls people to it with its promise of excitement and high-paying jobs.

NONMIGRANTS

Villagers who have remained in Hsin-hsing have had to adapt to the land problems that led others to migrate. Some—former landlords or rich peasants who have managed to accumulate capital—have established small local stores in the village and sell pesticides, fertilizer, or groceries. One family has established a rice mill, and another a small factory within the village where metal springs are fabricated on a contract basis for a machinery manufacturer. Both are strictly family enterprises, however, providing no work opportunities for other villagers. Several of the better-educated prereform landlords have taken local civil-service positions. All of these men supplement their income from the land by diversifying their economic interests at home.

Village families without adequate landholdings (the majority in Hsin-hsing) have turned to other sources of income in order to remain in the village. Some have sent members to the city to supplement the living they make from their small landholdings. Members of other families take seasonal jobs as farm laborers, work in local industries, or peddle goods or services in the local area.

Many residents now farm their land more intensively with short-term cash crops. Improvements in transportation over the last ten years have made vegetable cultivation for city markets feasible in the Hsin-hsing area. Labor-intensive truck farming is profitable, however, only when the family's labor pool is large enough to obviate cash payments for field labor. In addition, the growing of vegetables for market is a precarious enterprise; weather, plant disease, crop failure, and market glut all pose threats to the farmer. Thus, some village families have been unwilling to run the risk of converting to vegetable farming. Some who did run the risk succumbed, whereas others lack the labor needed to truck farm. In many cases, land-deficient households in these situations have emigrated to the cities as a last resort.

Table 7. *Place of Residence and Registration of Emigrants and Nonmigrants for Hsin-hsing Village, 1956–1966*

	Place of Residence			
Place of Registration	Hsin-hsing	Taipei	Elsewhere	Total Registered Population
Hsin-hsing:				
Male	236	46	25	—
Female	270	23	12	—
Total	506	69	37	612
Taipei:				
Male	—	96	—	—
Female	—	96	—	—
Total	—	192	—	192
Total resident population	506	261	37	—

Hsin-hsing Village Background

Over the last twenty-five years, Hsin-hsing village has been losing population steadily, but this loss is only partially reflected in the records of the township public office, where registrations show a relatively stable number of people.[6] (In this section and throughout the remainder of the chapter we use data collected in 1965–1966.) The registered population of the village was 609 people in 99 households (*hu*) in 1958, and 612 people in 112 households in 1966. In fact, although 612 people were registered in Hsin-hsing, only 506 actually lived there. The rest were living in the localities to which they had migrated (Table 7).

Within the village, families are grouped in the first instance by patrilineal kinship into lineages (*tsu*) or incipient lineages consisting of a few recently divided family units. The families within a lineage share a demonstrated common ancestor in the village itself. Virilocal marriage (the practice of couples traditionally living in the village of the male) perpetuates localization by surname. Although twelve surnames are represented in the village, four—Huang, Shih, K'ang, and Shen—account for some 80 percent of the population. There are more kin groups than surnames, however, since in certain cases resident families of the same surname are descended from two or more unrelated earlier settlers. Regardless of size, these *tsu* groups live in separate compounds or in house clusters within the village.

The *tsu* functions as a ceremonial group, drawing its members together for ancestor worship and life-crisis rituals. The *tsu* also has political importance. The more powerful *tsu* within the village form coalitions in an attempt to coordinate and control village affairs. Influential members mediate in conflicts within and between the lineages.[7] In addition, *tsu* coalitions control the internal politics of the village, and elected offices tend to be held by members of the larger *tsu*. That large *tsu* are considered influential can be seen from the fact that unrelated families who bear the same surname as an influential *tsu* try to identify themselves with the group in order to gain sociopolitical benefits and security that accrue to its members.

Unrelated families and individual families within the *tsu* do not by themselves wield power within the villages. But the family unit still stands as a source of security and is important in structuring relationships. Nuclear families predominate, there being sixty-five of this simple type as against twenty-nine stem and five joint families in the village. A nuclear family is converted to a stem family when a daughter-in-law is brought in for a son, and a stem family becomes joint as other sons marry. But inevitably the family breaks up into conjugal units, each starting anew as a nuclear family. In the wake of family division, however, mutual aid, cooperation in daily tasks, and ritual interaction among the component units persist for at least a generation.

Kinship is by no means the only basis for social relations within Hsin-hsing and the more extensive local system to which it belongs. A variety of voluntary associations draws unrelated families together and provides opportunities to develop friendships and relationships that cross kinship and even class lines. Hsin-hsing villagers participate in the farmers' association, public and private irrigation associations, cooperative agricultural labor teams, and such intervillage associations as the committee (drawing on twelve villages) that organizes the annual procession to honor the goddess Ma Tsu.

Moreover, recent developments have steadily diminished the significance of kinship in Hsin-hsing. The land-reform program of 1949–1953 expropriated some of the corporate and private landholdings of the lineages and the few local landlords; as a result, the position of the traditional landlord leaders within kin groups and in village politics was weakened. The Land Consolidation Program, which began in the early 1960s, eliminated a former basis for agricultural cooperation among kinsmen. This program redistributed the farmers' fragmented landholdings and provided them with blocks of land whose new locations draw farmers into different cooperative relationships that cross kin and village lines. The development of township-wide political factions is diminishing the importance of traditional bonds. And finally, the more frequent

Table 8. Migrant Units: Families and Persons Residing Apart from Their Families in Taipei and Hsin-hsing, 1965–1966

Category	Joint	Stem	Nuclear	Individual	Total
Hsin-hsing migrant units in Taipei	2	5	29	41	77
Migrant units that belong to *chia* with members residing in Hsin-hsing	0	0	5	41	—
Persons in the 77 Hsin-hsing migrant units in Taipei:					
Male	8	20	83	31	142
Female	8	15	86	10	119
Hsin-hsing residents in the *chia* to which migrant units belong:					
Male	0	0	13	78	91
Female	0	0	11	83	94
Total membership of *chia* with members residing in Taipei:					
Male	8	20	96	109	233
Female	8	15	97	93	213

Source: Field interviews.

intercession of government agencies and organizations in times of conflict has tended to undermine the importance of the *tsu* group in mediation.[8]

Hsin-hsing Migrants in Taipei

The first migrants from Hsin-hsing found work in Taipei as laborers in the Central Market area of Ch'eng-chung district. Within a few years of their arrival, several other Hsin-hsing men had joined them, attracted by their offers of help in obtaining jobs and housing. Over the years, the great majority of migrants to Taipei have taken jobs similar to those of the first migrants and settled in living quarters close to each other with the help of fellow villagers and kinsmen already in the city. As a result of this chain migration to Taipei and greater opportunities there, none of the Hsin-hsing migrants for the period 1945–1970 went to the closer cities of Taichung and Chang-hua (Table 1).

By 1965–1966, 261 natives of Hsin-hsing resided in Taipei (Table 7). Of this total, 220 fell into 36 family units (2 joint, 5 stem, and 29 nuclear); the remaining 41 Hsin-hsing migrants worked in Taipei while their families lived in Hsin-hsing. Five of these 36 family units considered to be based in

Table 9. Migrant units in Taipei with and without landholdings in Hsin-hsing, 1950 and 1965.

Migrant unit	Family type			
	Joint	Stem	Nuclear	Individual
1950				
Without land:				
Percent	0%	50%	21%	14%
Units	0	2	4	2
With land:				
Percent	100%	50%	79%	86%
Units	2	2	15	12
Total	2	4	19	14
1965				
Without land:				
Percent	0%	40%	34%	16%
Units	0	2	10	7
With land:				
Percent	100%	60%	66%	84%
Units	2	3	19	34
Total	2	5	29	41

Source: Interview and land records of the Land Bureau of Chang-hua county.

Taipei have an additonal 24 members, mostly children or parents, still residing in Hsin-hsing, where they maintain the families' landholdings (Table 8).[9]

Approximately three-quarters of Hsin-hsing migrants to Taipei between 1945 and 1969 operated land in the village at the time of their initial move, and in 1966, the same proportion still owned or rented some land in the village (Tables 5 and 9). The first migrants, those who moved during 1945–1950, operated less village land at the time of their departure than did subsequent migrants—an indication, as the migrants themselves suggest, that the economic situation of the earliest migrants was extremely serious (Table 5). Nevertheless, later migrants still feel that their landholdings were inadequate to meet family needs.

The move to Taipei is usually made piecemeal. In the typical case, the male family head or a grown son goes first to Taipei. The men move initially without their wives or families and send part of their earnings back to their families in the village. At the outset, they return often to the village to plant and harvest crops or to observe festivals or rituals. However, as time goes on, the family normally hires part-time farm labor to perform more and more of the agricultural activities, so that many men gradually make fewer trips to the village and limit their visits to the most important rituals, such as deaths and weddings and some of the major festivals—the village god's birthday, the Ma Tsu procession, and the New Year.

Over 85 percent of the villagers who have migrated to Taipei have remained. Single men usually return to the village to marry girls selected either by their parents with their agreement or, more rarely, by themselves in Taipei. In the latter "love matches," the girls almost always are migrants from the south, and the couple has asked a fellow villager or a matrilateral or affinal relative to serve as marriage broker. In either case, after the marriage, the groom immediately returns to his job, and usually within a few weeks or months, his wife joins him in the city.

After a period of adjustment to regular work, married migrants usually bring their families to live with them. In the typical case, the wife comes to Taipei six or seven years after her husband, accompanied in many cases by other members of the family. Sometimes the wife decides to move to the city after becoming suspicious of her husband's activities there. In such cases, the wife and younger children go to Taipei to "cut down on family expenses" by cooking and making a home for the man.

The move soon becomes established as permanent for many of the villagers whose families have joined them in the city. Nonetheless, the majority of the migrants retain their land in the village, oftentimes more for security than as an economic investment, since they usually derive little or no income from their land. Nineteen of the twenty-nine Taipei-based nuclear families have arranged for a kinsman (brother or parent) to tend their land in the village. These kinsmen retain most if not all of the proceeds from the land in return for their work. It is not unlikely that in holding onto their farmland, many families wish to be prepared for any contingency, such as the loss of jobs or the coming of another war. None of the heads of these families was prepared to say that farmland had been retained because he himself intended to return to live and work in the village someday. In fact, three of these families have sold a portion of their land: one to build a house in Taipei, another to buy a delivery-cart engine, and the third to pay for the marriage of a son.

Whether or not farmland is retained, none of the Taipei-based families has sold its Hsin-hsing living quarters, even when all of its members live in Taipei and seldom return to the village. These rooms are sealed, used for storage rooms by the migrants or by relatives in the village, or lent (normally without charge) to village relatives. A house, and land if it is considered ancestral, seems to be retained largely for symbolic reasons. Selling it would signify the final breaking of ties.

Eventually, most of the Taipei-based migrant families, including most

Table 10. Occupations of Migrants from Hsin-hsing in Taipei, by Sex,
        1965–1966

Occupation	Related to Activities in the Taipei Central Market		Unrelated to the Taipei Central Market		Total	
	Male	Female	Male	Female	Male	Female
Cart driver (laborer)	34	0	4	0	38	0
Pedicab driver	0	0	9	0	9	0
Taxi driver	0	0	1	0	1	0
Shop Clerk	4	0	1	0	5	0
Factory worker	0	0	1	8	1	8
Vegetable gardener	1	0	0	0	1	0
Apprentice	1	0	0	0	1	0
Craftsman	0	0	1	0	1	0
Carpenter	0	0	4	0	4	0
Rag collector	0	0	1	0	1	0
Peddler	5	1	2	0	7	1
Shopkeeper (merchant)	5	0	3	0	8	0
Total	50	1	27	8	77	9

Source: Field interviews.

of those who retain their village land, become settled in their work and return to the village only on special occasions such as the New Year or large village festivals. Migrants usually do not return home to observe ancestor worship, nor do they worship in Taipei. The frequency of visits to Hsin-hsing seems to be based primarily on the presence of family connections or landholdings in the village. Home visits are necessarily limited by the expense—the costs of the trip itself and the attendant loss of income. In addition, the work of many migrants does not permit them to come and go as they please.

For the majority of the migrants who arrived in Taipei prior to 1960, work is in the service-type jobs that were readily available in the 1950s (Tables 6 and 10). Those who came in the 1960s, when village families had grown used to the idea of sending their young to work in Taipei, more commonly hold factory jobs; and this is particularly true of females. The number of factory jobs increased substantially in the early 1960s, and at the same time, the availability of more lucrative service-type jobs decreased. Younger people therefore often could find jobs more easily than could their elders, whose family responsibilities necessitated wages higher than those that factories or shops generally pay to unskilled workers.

In 1966, about 65 percent of the male migrants held jobs in the vegetable section of the Taipei Central Market or connected in some way with the vegetable market (Table 10). Only four of the thirty-eight cart drivers were working in jobs not connected with the vegetable market, and two of these four men worked for a lumberyard nearby. Thirty-four delivered vegetables to the individual vegetable stalls within the market, from the Wanhua freight station to the market, or from the market to the customers of the wholesale vegetable merchants. The heavy concentration of Hsinhsing villagers in cart driving is attributable to the postwar expansion and reorganization of the Central Market. However, after the first migrants got started, they helped their fellow villagers and kinsmen find similar jobs. In most instances, later migrants came to Taipei expecting to obtain work in the Central Market, even if only to deliver vegetables on a small handcart.

Five of the eight shopkeepers among Hsin-hsing migrants sell vegetables wholesale inside the Central Market. Two of these men came to Taipei during the late 1940s and became clerks for established merchants at extremely low wages. Gradually they learned the trade and with accumulated savings opened their own businesses inside the market when costs were still moderate and space readily available. A third shopkeeper began work as a clerk upon arrival in Taipei during the early period, but he became impatient and left this job to become a cart driver at a much higher wage. Unlike other migrants who began their careers in this same way, he managed to open a business in the late 1950s. The remaining two Hsin-hsing merchants are younger men, in their thirties, who recently opened businesses in the market after first working as clerks. Of all the migrants, the five merchants are the most financially secure today.

These merchants and the men who work as cart drivers and clerks in and around the Central Market see each other regularly during their working hours. They usually start work shortly after 1:00 A.M., when the vegetables begin to arrive at the market, and end at about 11:00 A.M.. Most men do not go home immediately after work; some cart drivers remain in the market and do extra work for merchants, while others—the majority— relax by talking, joking, gambling, and sometimes drinking together. They finally leave the market for home sometime after noon.

Home for the majority of the migrants is in Wan-hua in the Shuangyüan district, or in the vicinity of the Central Market in Ch'eng-chung district. Both districts are inhabited by large numbers of people from other counties or municipalities in Taiwan and by people who have generally poor educational backgrounds. On the basis of inferences from the P'u-yen township data, we would assume a great proportion of these people are rural-to-urban migrants.

Migrants usually attempt to find living quarters near kinsmen or at least

*Table 11. Distribution of Hsin-hsing Migrant Units by District and
Surname, Taipei, 1965–1966*

Surname	Shuang-yüan	Ch'eng-chung	Other Five Districts	Total
Huang	48	12	19	79
Shen	40	10	2	52
K'ang	29	10	8	47
Shih	6	25	6	37
Li	22	—	—	22
Wang	—	12	1	13
Others	1	—	10	11
Total	146	69	46	261
Total percent	56	26	18	100

Source: Field interviews.

other villagers. As a result, most Hsin-hsing natives live in residential clusters of fellow villagers and kinsmen, and even the outliers usually live within visiting distance (Table 11). Migrants who live outside the two central districts tend to be from Hsin-hsing's smallest kin groups or from isolated families. A few of these outliers are young persons working in factories or shops and living in quarters furnished by the employer. However, most of the migrants who do not live in the two central districts either have independent jobs or work in small businesses that are totally unrelated to the Central Market. Not one of them works in the Central Market. Some live and work with affinal relatives, and others with natives of P'u-yen township outside Hsin-hsing.

Seven of the Taipei-based families own their own houses. In several instances, two or more families of cart drivers have jointly rented a large apartment; each family is assigned a bedroom, while the sitting room and other facilities are shared. In at least one such case, the sharing families, all Huangs, are agnates. In virtually all such cases, the Hsin-hsing migrants happily note that living together in this manner is like being in a large family situation once again. Most families, however, rent tiny places, usually no more than one very small room, and share cooking, washing, and toilet facilities with all the other families in the rented house. Within a particular house, families are seldom kinsmen or even from the same village or area; conveniently located and inexpensive houses are scarce, and the migrants must rent what they can find.

Integration into City Life

To what extent have Hsin-hsing migrants continued to rely on kin- and village-based networks to satisfy their needs in the city? We have seen that almost all of the migrants depended upon village-derived connections to take care of their immediate needs for employment and housing. As a result, the majority have jobs in the Central Market, which has natural centripetal consequences. The vegetable merchants have daily contacts with their fellow migrants. The cart drivers work and relax together every day; the gossip in which they engage tends to foster a community of interest and makes the Central Market the communication node of the Hsin-hsing community and, to a lesser extent, of the migrant community from Chang-hua county as a whole.

Within the market, many of these people have organized themselves into groups somewhat akin to guilds and *pang*, which the government allows to function as monopolies in the interest of orderly market operation. The first such group organized was the Vegetable Merchants' Association. In order to maximize their profits, merchants needed two kinds of predictable labor services: delivery of wholesale produce to their stands in the market, and delivery of large loads of produce to major buyers outside the market. The association's first efforts, therefore, were directed toward organizing workers into two stable labor groups to perform these services. Migrants from Chang-hua county and particularly from Hsin-hsing dominate these groups. Over half of the members of one group, which has a contractual arrangement with the Vegetable Merchants' Association, are from Hsin-hsing, and most of these men are from one patrilineage. The other group has the tacit recognition of, but not an official contract with, the association. It was organized by a Hsin-hsing villager, and more than half of its members are from the village.

The preponderance of Hsin-hsing migrants in the two labor groups is not surprising; men from Hsin-hsing were among the earliest arrivals in the market, formed the largest village grouping there compared with any other single identifiable place, and were most familiar with the vegetable merchants. In addition, at the time the two labor groups were formed, many of the merchants' relationships still were based on kinship or village identity or both. It was reasonable then, that when organization occurred, such criteria defined the membership. Given these conditions, one might have expected to find a much higher proportion of Hsin-hsing migrants in these groups. Since their arrival in the city, though, all of the migrants have developed new and intense reciprocal relationships with people not from Hsin-hsing—usually also migrants—on the basis of such shared experiences as being employed in the same market or living in the same area. Over time, many of these bonds have come to be considered more effective bases for developing the trust and cooperation necessary for the effectiveness of the groups than the ones brought from the village. As a result, when positions became available in the groups, they began to be offered to city-based friends rather than to kinsmen or fellow villagers.

Despite the admission of "outsiders" to the groups, however, Hsin-hsing workers continue to exhibit a sense of unity among themselves within the market. Along with nongroup villagers, later arrivals form an informal coalition that tries to protect its members against police harassment. The coalition's success depends not only on sheer numbers but also on support from influential merchants, who sometimes help when they feel orderly market operation might be affected by problems among the laborers. The coalition's performance has varied over the years, but Hsin-hsing laborers view membership in the coalition as a means of obtaining a degree of security within the market, and so it remains an active grouping.

Outside the market, however, the Hsin-hsing laborers have failed to organize themselves into a cohesive mutual-aid group. Nor have they joined with other migrants from the Lu-kang or P'u-yen township areas to form a formal regional organization. This is partly because they have only a small population of natives in Taipei, and only a few potential members from these places command resources, and furthermore, because they do not feel much threatened. Nevertheless, laborers do report that they are looked down upon by Taipei natives because they are "outsiders" (ch'u-wai jen)—a term apparently applied to anyone from outside the immediate area of Taipei. And, they believe that this attitude, along with their limited personal relationships with influential people, is responsible for their failure to secure government welfare benefits and services such as credit, legal aid, and protection.

Thus, despite the limited threats directed against the migrants as people from a particular place, their belief that they are discriminated against provides a founding principle for a county-based association in Taipei. The group was organized in the early 1960s by several politically ambitious men from Chang-hua county who, in order to develop a clientele and following, used these beliefs and "t'ungism" to recruit members from among the large number of Chang-hua migrants in the city. Suggesting that ties based on a common county of origin were meaningful links that implied acts of reciprocity, these men promised prospective members patronage in exchange for political support.

Almost all the Hsin-hsing migrants responded to these recruitment pledges and joined the Chang-hua County (Regional) Association. Few, however, report having derived benefits from their membership. The association leaders' promises of aid appear to be met only at election time, when the association acts as a viable group representing the community of migrants. At all other times, it serves primarily as an arena in which its more successful members organize alliances they can translate into social, economic and political advantages. However, since the Hsin-hsing laborers usually manage to organize relationships through their associational activity only with people whose resources are as limited as their own, their membership fails to provide them with any beneficial ties to patrons or power brokers.

As a result, the only groups to which the laborers belong that enable them to counter threats directed against them are their occupational ties. But these associations are exclusively economic in interest and proletarian in membership and provide them limited opportunities outside the Central Market. Thus, the laborers believe that their most promising avenue to success in the city is close and effective relationships with the Hsin-hsing merchants, whom they hope will call upon their ties with people of higher standing on the laborers' behalf.

The merchants, for their part, are integrating themselves into Taipei by means of their increasing participation in sociopolitical associations. They take care, however, to preserve their village-based relationships which enable them to make a contribution to the leaders of their new groupings and help ensure that they will remain welcome among them. Many of these associations serve primarily as a vehicle for the more ambitious, and the merchants are recruited into them in order to exert influence on the lower-class migrants and thereby promote the leaders' political interests. Thus, the continuing ties maintained between the Hsin-hsing laborers and the Hsin-hsing merchants are mutually useful. On the one hand, they bolster and secure the merchants' positions among their new associates, and on the other hand, they provide the laborers with an indirect access to power. The two groups of migrants therefore continue to depend on each other.

In addition, village-based relationships continue to have significance within the two distinct groups of migrants. For example, laborers frequently lend each other small amounts of money without any interest, or join each other's moneylending or credit clubs. At the time of a wedding or other festive occasion, when many people must be entertained, they will offer their services as hosts. And often they will send *hung-pao* (a gift of money wrapped in red paper) on the occasion of a wedding, even when they are not planning to attend the dinner for which such a gift is obligatory.

The explanation they give for this practice is that it is done to make *jen-ch'ing*, a term meaning "the expression of good will or feeling." The gesture, however, is more than merely expressive, since laborers anticipate that the gift will be reciprocated when they celebrate a similar occasion. A migrant, in fact, when he uses the compound *jen-ch'ing* in speaking of its occurrence in his relationship with another, always uses it with the word *ch'ien*, meaning "to owe." Thus, the practice is used as a means of creating personal-obligation ties with others.

The main reason laborers seem to take this care in maintaining their relationships with one another is that in the city, an uncertainty exists about such relationships. The migrants no longer live in a small community in which residential concentration, socioreligious and political activities, and formal organizations draw them together, foster reciprocal relations, and exert pressure on individuals to conform to expected norms of behavior. As a result, although kinsmen and fellow villagers represent a source of help and security that most likely can be tapped in times of need, these relationships are considered voluntary, not obligatory, and laborers believe they must be nurtured.

In addition, the laborers believe it is necessary to seek out people other than kinsmen and fellow villagers with whom they can ally themselves and on whom they can depend. Most frequently, they establish friendships with workmates or neighbors, also usually migrants. At the outset, these relationships are casual and primarily involve occasional get-togethers to eat and drink. Over time, many increase in intensity and evolve into close and cooperative relationships involving exchanges of goods and services in both ritual and nonritual contexts. On festive occasions, friends are entertained, and at the time of a wedding or death, friends help out with gifts of money. In additon, friends frequently visit each other's homes informally, and in time of financial need, furnish short-term loans without interest.

These relationships, however, like village-based ones, involve only voluntary actions of individuals or families. Friends, therefore, in order to be more certain of each other's potentiality as a source of aid, will sometimes organize themselves into a sworn-brotherhood group. Migrants believe that such groupings unite people by encouraging subscription to a common set of norms and by introducing a degree of obligation into relationships. Thus, they tend to guarantee that aid will be forthcoming when needed, since the sanctions of the group can be mobilized to oblige individual sworn brothers to fulfill their obligations.

Despite the utilitarian quality of these groups, the emotional ties of friendship define and characterize the relations among and between its members. Not all sworn-brotherhood groups, however, are organized as an outgrowth of warm and close friendships. Sometimes such groups are formed solely to maximize the socioeconomic and political opportunities of their participants; friendship may be used as a vechicle to enroll members and solidify their loyalties, but participants are recruited selectively, with consideration given to the potential contribution of each individual to the group.

All five of the Hsin-hsing Central Market merchants belong to one such group, which includes among its twenty-eight members a Taipei city councilwoman whose father is a national assemblyman, the neighborhood chief (*lin-chang*) of Ch'eng-chung district, a member of the board of the Ch'eng-chung Cooperative Bank, the head of the Chang-hua Regional Association, and the vice-chief of the Provincial Water Bureau. During the proceedings that culminated in the formation of the group, the anticipated contributions of the different members were articulated; the merchants were to develop a following for the politically ambitious "brothers" in exchange for economic and sociopolitical favors. Notwithstanding this frank statement of expected advantage, the group does attempt to foster camaraderie by holding dinner parties at members' homes every third month, and members participate in each other's lifecycle rituals in their role as fictive brothers.

Joint participation in the sworn-brotherhood group and overlapping membership in other groupings have reinforced preexisting ties between the merchants and encouraged closer relations. Since they compete for both customers and farmers' agents, from whom they buy their produce, they previously maintained only rather formal relationships. Their close and intense relationships usually were not with their fellow merchants, but with others whom they had met since their arrival in the city. As they have become more involved in associational activities, however, they have had the opportunity to meet and relate with each other in an arena other than the one in which they normally compete. As a result, they have developed closer and more cooperative relationships, and village and kinship ties continue to have meaning for them.

Summary and Conclusions

Earlier we saw marked differences between the people who move from villages to nearby urban towns and cities and those who move to the larger and more distant cities. Unlike Speare, we found that these migrants to large cities did not have above-average educations and were not better off financially; on the contrary, they had below-average educations and usually were the more economically depressed residents of the areas from which they migrated.[10]

The variance between these two findings may be due in part to differences between large cities such as Taichung (the focus of Speare's work) and urban-industrial centers such as Taipei, the historical fact of the influx of mainlanders into these latter cities, and a host of other factors. Taiwan's fine systems of communication and transportation make the most distant city easily accessible. A chain of relationships with earlier migrants, like the one that drew Chinese from southeast China to Southeast Asian countries over the past several hundred years, attracted the Hsin-hsing-area migrants to large, distant cities. Most of these migrants therefore were not part of the stepwise migration stream in which rural migrants first move to urban towns—perhaps taking the jobs of townspeople who have migrated to cities—and later move to the cities.[11] Instead, the great majority of migrants from Hsin-hsing and the three other villages we considered emigrated directly to the distant industrial centers, where well-paying employment is available for people with limited resources.

Within the city, the migrants from one village, Hsin-hsing, do not form a cohesive urban community, but they are bound by certain formal and informal ties. Most work in related occupations within the Central Market. When occupational organization occurred there, particularistic criteria determined the core membership of the favored labor groups, and Hsin-hsing villagers dominate the groups. Membership in these groups, however, is not based solely on ascribed bonds of common origin; many men were recruited into the groups in later years on the basis of common experience. Nevertheless, as the largest single village grouping within the market, Hsin-hsing laborers have organized an informal coalition that actively protects and promotes their economic interests.

Outside the market, the Hsin-hsing migrants neither have a large enough population nor are sufficiently wealthy or influential to organize an active t'ungist group. In fact, the only regional level with a large enough population to support a t'ung-hsiang group in Taipei is the county from which the migrants emigrated. The county-based association that was organized, however, is seen as essentially irrelevant by most laborers, since it neither helps them to counter the discrimination directed against them nor helps them to operate within the institutions of the city and the wider society. The association is, however, seen as an active and viable group by its more successful migrant members, who use it to create advantage for themselves outside the group.

The sociopolitical integration of migrants into city life depends, then, to a large degree upon class. The Hsin-hsing laborers for the most part lack meaningful relationships with people of higher standing within the city, and many of the problems they face are not easily solved. The Hsin-hsing merchants have extended their relationships upward in the city's social and political structure and have increased their ability to maneuver socially, politically, and economically. The two groups of migrants nevertheless continue to maintain relationships with each other in order to satisfy their needs and to promote their interests. These relationships, not surprisingly, tend to resemble patron-client models rather than alliances of equals. The merchants offer to exercise indirect influence on those with power to help the laborers meet certain economic or personal threats. In exchange, the laborers offer a clientele and political following, thus providing the means by which the merchants can secure cooperation from those in power.

Thus, kinship- and village-based relationships continue to be significant for most Hsin-hsing migrants, even though institutional supports that help ensure unity and cooperation in the village do not function in the city. These relationships, however, are less structured in the city and are not oriented around the group. Instead, they operate mainly on the family level and on a selective and voluntary basis. Nevertheless, the ties of mutual identification that are reinforced by overlapping social networks and modes of social participation—especially those stemming from related occupational activities—function to hold the majority of this migrant group together as a quasi community within the city of Taipei.

Notes

* This chapter was discussed in *The Chinese City Between Two Worlds*, Mark Elvin and G. William Skinner, eds. (Stanford, Calif.: Stanford University Press, 1974), and in "Agricultural Development in Taiwan" by Bernard Gallin in *Common Ground* 4, #3 (Fall 1978).
1. George W. Barclay, *Colonial Development and Population in Taiwan* (Princeton, N.J.: Princeton University Press, 1954), p. 13. Department of Civil Affairs, *Monthly Bulletin of Registration Statistics of Taiwan* 2, no. 1 (January 1967): 10.
2. Andrew Collver, Alden Speare, Jr. and Paul K. C. Liu, "Local Variations of Fertility in Taiwan," *Population Studies* 20, no. 3 (March 1967): 329–42.
3. Hsien-jen Chu, "An Exploratory Study of Internal Migration in Taiwan," (Ph.D. diss., University of Florida, 1966), p. 92.
4. Data drawn from family records in the public office include the total population of the four settlements, numbers of migrants to each place, and age and educational background at the time of migration. Official family records are known to be inaccurate in certain respects; for instance, a certain portion of migrants register late or not at all. However, since there is no reason to assume a biased distribution of these errors, a comparative analysis on the basis of these statistics is justified.

5. Alden Speare, Jr., "The Determinants of Rural to Urban Migration in Taiwan," (Ph.D. diss., University of Michigan, 1969), pp. 29–30; and Paul K. C. Liu, "Population Redistribution and Development in Taiwan," (paper prepared for the Conference on Economic Development of Taiwan, Taipei, June 19–29, 1967), pp. 213–15.
6. For a more complete ethnographic study of this village, see Bernard Gallin, *Hsin-Hsing, Taiwan: A Chinese Village in Change* (Berkeley: University of California Press, 1966).
7. For a discussion of the problems of conflict resolution in the Hsin-hsing area, see Bernard Gallin, "Mediation in Changing Chinese Society in Rural Taiwan," *Journal of Asian and African Studies* 2, no. 2 (April 1967): 77–90.
8. Bernard Gallin, "Political Factionalism and Its Impact on Chinese Village Social Organization in Taiwan," in *Local-Level Politics*, Marc J. Swartz, ed. (Chicago: Aldine, 1968), pp. 377–400.
9. The term "Taipei-based family unit" refers to a coresident group of related persons that includes at least one conjugal couple and that resides in Taipei. In addition, while most members of these 36 family units are officially registered in Taipei, 13 of them still have 50 of their members registered in Hsin-hsing.
10. Speare, "The Determinants of Rural to Urban Migration," pp. 52–61.
11. Ibid., p. 44.